ATALANTA FUGIENS

The Devil's Crown

Key to the mysteries of Robert Cochrane's Craft

Being volume four of the Star Crossed Serpent

Shani Oates

Published by

Mandrake of Oxford

PO Box 250

OXFORD

OX1 1AP (UK)

Printed on acid free paper certification from three leading environmental organizations: the Forest Stewardship Council™ (FSC®), the Sustainable Forestry Initiative® (SFI®) and the Programme for the Endorsement of Forestry Certification (PEFC™)

Other books by Shani Oates and available from Mandrake:

Tubelo's Green Fire: Mythos, Ethos, Female, Male and Priestly Mysteries of The Clan of Tubal Cain, isbn 978-1-906958-07-7

The Arcane Veil: Witchcraft and Occult Science from the People of the Dark-ages to the People of Goda, of the Clan of Tubal Cain.
978-1-906958-35-0 (£25/$40 hbk)

Contents

1
The Mark of Cain: Devil's Crown

"Night, the beloved. Night, when words fade and things come alive. When the destructive analysis of day is done, and all that is truly important becomes whole and sound again. When man reassembles his fragmentary self and grows with the calm of a tree."[1]

Above his brow, three curling flame-like strands suggest the fire-brand of shin, the triple fire and triple horns of this eponymous and eternal wanderer (the sense of eternal seeker). Referred to as *'Pashupati'*,[2] this Cainite figure is sometimes compared to an occulted entity akin to Methuselah named 'Agrimus, the Curled One,' first born of Lilith and Adam, according to Jewish Folklore. He also had knowledge of metal craft to bind spirits.

These and other glorious medieval occultisms continue to thrive within our current era. Once the ancient preserve of their native cultures, they have blossomed through fruitful operation and are beheld as inner-mysteries within numerous western traditions. Cross-cultural diversity, as a 'given' key to the mysteries, is typified therein. Agrimus is a daemon whose role as the ancient of ancients, traverses all spiritual and physical realms thereto aid and guard the heroes of the human race, advancing the species by default. The Soul receives and processes this information within the confines of the cultural sheath traversed in Wyrd.

However, despite the eponymous tutelary spirit of **The Clan**, the **People of Goda** do not draw its mysteries, mythos, teachings or beliefs from the confines of the Judeo/Christian dogma, nor from superstitions popular to certain other traditions. Rather it draws from myths and legends that are sourced in Northern regions. The quotation above, is from a study into the origins of the personage of Cain, one that flags all cognate associations, and cultural forms. Within our particular Tradition, we have elements pertinent to British folklore much overlooked in the current occult world. Bowers lamented upon the favour found in the 'eastern star,' the strand of belief that sourced the 'Western' magickal tradition and all filtrations of Judaeo-Christian magics and cultic factions.

He favoured that tradition not and looked to more northern climes, the lands of his ancestors, to those who stirred his blood and inspired his process of anamnesis. He understood better than most the significance of symbolism and the needs of succinct application. The mocking Fool, the Jestor's jape, the Grim Herlekin.—Divil's all, bearing Her Flame, barbs of the thorn, tines of the royal beast she hunts and slays. Tangs of the staff he holds aloft, She, as the divine feminine, is the Fire to his Light. Sunna—daag. Her flaming shin is the Tiara of the 'Triple Mothers' and the Three Queens of our Tradition, whose gift to the King (root of Qyn meaning ruler/monarch) ultimately manifests as the 'Divill's Crown.'

♦ All Father Cain and Tubal Cain

Very much a metaphysical state of being and not necessarily a physical 'mark,' as it were. Where it does appear as a tattoo, it is something that comes through tradition and family. Within those who consider themselves to be the 'Children of Cain,' is a dormant gene, which is deeply receptive to the spirit of the 'true mark.' Becoming active 'through desire, the first of all created things,' it is seen and acknowledged by those who share that path or have knowledge of it. By the mark, shall we know each family, and 'be blessed' in their Companie.

Our species alone has the sole preserve, in privileged possession of this most uniquely formed stigmata. Its seed potential has never been fully realised, for it is not a sign of an intellectual elite, as some would have it. To each family is given an indelible sign, perhaps a scar or tattoo, an outward acknowledgement of an irrefutable commitment already given. Perhaps all souls will eventually evolve through this mark as they journey forward, fulfilling individual argosies.

There is a natural and etymological link between the words, 'mark' and 'boundary,' that may suggest how the former denotes inclusive protection within the latter; a sense epitomised by the rune: *Þurisaz*, curiously known as the devil's rune!

> *"And the Lord said unto him, therefore whosoever slayeth Cain, vengeance shall be taken on him sevenfold. And the Lord set a mark upon Cain, lest any finding him should kill him." (Genesis 4:15 KJV)*

Cain's mark finds mention in the Anglo-Saxon Epic, Beowulf, where its pronunciation may be noted as: *Óowth* - 'oath' to the ear. This can mean a sign, mark, banner, remembrance, omen, warning, token, ensign, standard/guiden, or miracle, adding further credence to a presumed connection between the Mark of Cain and the act of devotion, a surrender to, an allegiance whereby the emblem of aegis is lauded. As an all-encompassing concept of mark, oath and proof, it provokes the notion of being 'touched' by God; where one given the 'sign,' is by extension, a divine emissary.

Nonetheless, Cain's alleged fratricidal depravity has served civilised society particularly well. Prejudicial ontological judgment projected onto our humanity, certain flaws that ironically developed the notion of an archetypal scapegoat. Bound eternally to the 'mark,' Cain was offered up, the recalcitrant parody for anarchy and chaos, deeply patented as the primal 'other.' Universal comparison of this critique attracts significant typologies in error; first and foremost, is the presumption of sin. Labelled indelibly of that same ilk, humankind continuously turns its staid and judgmental filial eye, casting the shadow of condemnation and absent of objective perception. This fickle megalomania of the masses, obligingly turns the cyclopean eye ever outwards, seeking the horizon furthest from themselves. The arid landscape of the scapegoat looms brightly across their kaleidoscopic myopia; painful icy shards cut deeply into the heart of our humanity, blinding the seeker inwards, shattering myriad visions that petrify those devoid of an inner compass to guide them true. Deep within the subconscious realms of Mythopoeia, Tubal Cain haunts us as the Titanic, ante-diluvium progeny of Cain. All who carry 'that' mark find reference even in those most ancient of days, where Gilgamesh, Enkidu and all such heroes, would dare to blaze the torch of hope through the dark trials of sacrifice, burning the lie and all false despair on that eternal dawn of all becoming.

As 'mythical progenitor' and benefactor of the human race; his inflaming spirit hearkens, singing all souls to its dance of light, the fire burns best and brightest where the hearth stone holds kith and kin to its homage. Across much of the ancient world, sacred texts reveal the poignant tenets of all civilising arts, of military skills and pastoral sustenance. Divine kingship instigated the Law, the Credo by which all we hold in Faith today as manna for the inner soul, annealed in Tubelo's blackened forge. Nomadic Clans record a history replete with feuds and condemnation of the 'Other,' the exilic wanderer, innovator and adversary of stasis and the lie. Simple yet complex relationships bonded the Word, generating the honourable titles of 'Brother' and 'Sister,' though not in our modern usage or terminology but as those united within the divine spark shared by all in awareness of the Self, wherein the self is understood as the cause rather than the purpose of God's existence here on earth.

All Creation, at once became perceived as obedient to an illusion, that since remains upheld by fear and intolerance. Change must ever be the medium of need, resistance of desire. Wyrd thus determines the choices we are destined to make, whence all surrenders to the One. As liberator and opener of the ways, the arcane psychopomp wields the staff of the Pilgrim, the Fool and the humble Wanderer. The world has meted its judgment upon those who follow not the Crooked Path towards the Ship of Fools, but hearken instead the elusive Piper in the 'Charivari' of the would-be damned. The mission is inimical to those who would open their eyes to a clearer world, yet, in paradox, becoming what is anathema to it. An astute collaboration en-souls the root of CTC's aspirated ideal, ultimately finding expression through its 'mission' statement and through its evolution: the gift of its unfaltering Egregore.

Roy Bowers doggedly avowed his belief concerning the inescapable actuality of a conscious shift from one reality to another. Describing that paradox as the leap from one illusion: *'for what might be a greater illusion still…'*[3] Declaring his frustration in the culpability of humanity, he hoped that:

> *"…one day, someone is going to kick over the scenery, then we will all see the bare brick walls of the theatre.*[4]

We reach out in hope, to see beyond those flickering shadows, seeking the light; all the while, there, lurking in the dark, they yet remain, nought but oblique shimmers, shards of dull echoes. In this gloomy Mauve Zone, twilight beckons all dancing shades over many thresholds into somnambulistic dreamscapes, traversed by eyes cast upwards, flickering, entranced by the nimbus, reflected, retinal burn.

Do we interpret our visions encountered here as shaman, or priests? Can we be certain these roles are even creatively distinct in order that we might come to know the intrinsic virtue of either before being able to appreciate its combination? Perhaps *who* the grail serves, is the perennial conundrum. The nature of proof may be comprehended through participation alone. On this, Bowers adamantly wrote not of generic 'faith,' but 'of' Faith. And that 'proof,' *is* apprehended in participation of its disciplines thereof.

In our journeying, our questing through the Maze, we leave 'behind' something of ourselves at each gate we cross; yet, by way of compensation and balance, we also carry 'forward' an integral principle of its virtue. We leave behind all that is faded and worn, outmoded and abandoned for lack of service to that cause, serving as they did, the shackle of ignorance; an ill-fated mode. What we take forward, is hope, wisdom, choice and determination; all in that Faith.

Silence is the language of the gods. Or rather, in silence we may yet hear their call. In the texture of silence, there is knowledge for those who can recognize it. In silence, all sounds are in repose; all thoughts, are stillness; in space, is all fullness; in absence, there is presence. Consciousness is about an informed choice of awareness. The kaleidoscope shifts by degrees, and as the pattern changes, so does light, mood, sound and movement in tandem to the dance of our individual psyche.

Silence: the awe-full dread places. Silence: the deep breath of the all, we all respond in perfect harmony to the echo of our selves, the true reflection of the other, the voice without is also within. Each corporeal existence devolves humanity, and yet where it communes with the 'Other,' our evolution finds security. We are all here to learn, and to be with others, as kith, as kin, in Companie, and alone, with the alone: To 'know thyself,' is true gnosis indeed.

Silence is for the soul, communion for the spirit, and social intercourse for our humanity. Three times maketh the charm. This concept known to many is familiar in the most magickal sense. Both John (E.J. Jones) and Roy Bowers asserted silence as the purest vehicle for the building and adept manipulation of virtue; so it is inspiring indeed to see these maxims actualized. Moreover, universal familiarity awards the deepest validations of their testament to Truth.

> *"As you know, our methods are different, and to me they are meditational aids, builders of atmosphere, not commands to the super-consciousness. We hardly have any speaking at all, since after a certain point it gets in the way. We have chants, series of words and all that, but they are rarely used once things get moving. In fact I would find anyone who insisted on voicing words a nuisance"* and *"where you would use words as a key to the transformation of basic power, we again use actions."*[5]

♦ ## Devil's Advocate?

> *"Magic is only a by-product of the search for Truth, and holds an inferior position to Truth. Magic, that is the development of total will, is a product of the soul in its search for ultimate knowledge."*[6]

Providence honours all who seek to know more. Another man, strongly convicted in his Faith, with whom sacred space has been shared, likewise attuned to Truth, readily accepted our sense of it as comparable to his own. Fundamentally, 'we are all one.' A Sufi Master the Grand Sheik Ahmed Dede shared with us, the simple yet profound reality of the living stream. During a private Dhikir, he exclaimed, *"Many rivers run to the sea,"* he said, *"but we are only a stream and not the ocean".*

Perfect! And how true.

There are many ways to find Truth and not one of us may claim our path as definitive. It is beyond multi-faith, beyond tolerance for alternate creeds. As Doreen Valiente said (roughly paraphrased) 'the things that unite us, are stronger than the things that separate us.' This is not advocating that anyone should fling wide their doors to reveal all the dark and dusty secrets bereft and forlorn. Caution must prevail until everyone is able to see these truths. Until then, those of us who can, must seek to assist others to that strength of purpose, pushing back their boundaries, until they disappear.

Many good people suffer immense hardship and prejudice because they would not abjure their stream, nor in fact their faith; others fall easily, failing to recognise the similarities in the honest simplicity and liberation of a Godhead that is a Singularity. Named for 'Fate,' or Truth, it brooks no compromise but meets fear, head on. Only ignorance engenders mistrust. Culture, race, creed and politics all serve the state well (viz à viz—maintaining the status quo); whilst we immerse ourselves in the symptoms of corruption, the cause of it thrives, and heartily so. Engaged in what separates us, global genocide removes them.

Gaia girds her loins in readiness. No, wait! Perhaps all is not so grim as it may appear? Hindu temples brim with devotion; and we remember where, in a nearby monastery, a monk so beautiful ministers spiritual honey to needy souls, a healing balm in a vacuous world. Truly, in 'good' faith, anyone should be able to visit a church, temple, mosque, synagogue or sacred grove and find truth there. Religion had always properly meant 'to bind back,' that is, to a faith or belief held in continuous tradition. It is certainly not something picked up at weekends and put down again when otherwise engaged or distracted. As Sister Wendy so eloquently put it: *"Praying does not cease when you get up off your knees."*

Nor should it be hide-bound to a specific season or rite, Sabbath or holy day. Reality requires constant contact! Within The Clan, there is always at least one member in full time observance, on research sabbaticals, planning & creating all workings for the future ahead. Empty gestures just don't catch or hold the interest of the 'other.' No matter how theatrical or impressive, only fools and spectators will be so glamoured; never the gods.

Not to saunter here; we should all serve. Clan leaders, mindful of duty, and law, will eventually take their place as beloved and revered Elders; but only once all is successfully conveyed and held firmly within the grasp of another to carry forth the baton. Thereafter, they remain secure in a non-elective position, accessible even after death, in one form or another, of the spiritual, but not always of spirit. Of high regard and inestimable esteem, they are not to be discarded, or ignored. On a cosmic scale, we are all threads, wound upon Her Distaff. As individuals, our threads bind themselves to others, they trace descent and ascent, to and from our being. Knots may form at nodes within the matrix of life, the blood and bone of humanity.

But as the Folk, or People, we grow as branches from the central core of our tree. From that trunk, an Egregoric community stands, a pillar of bark and sinew, connected to its point of origin, at its 'Source.' Each family tree is maintained through its roots, grounded as they are deep within the earth. Each tree, unless en-fleshed with the spiritual Egregore of the Clan or Family, will wither and decay. Wica, by contrast, is a net of nodes and junctions, self-perpetuating *ad finitum* through each linear Initiate. A Craft Tradition is formed of several roots that create its trunk.

Above this rooted forest, the canopy of leaves dance and sway in the light they bathe in, each species of tree absorbing the pure virtue of Truth, conveyed through photosynthesis to nourish and maintain the vitality, the virtue of its kind. And so it is with Tradition, each according to their own, all drawing from the source, and all alongside one another. Separate, distinct, no homogeneity, but forming a splendid deciduous forest to reflect the beautiful glory of diversity. Blessed is this graft, enjoined within the 'source,' a most profound and inexpressible gift. The nearest articulation would be peace, or bliss, in the fullest and truest sense. To risk all and lose this, is indeed 'girt terror and fearful dread,' unless of course there is a dearth of belief or experience. To be 'cast out,' a fate worse than death, is to be with the dead, without hope of the quick. For this most profound of reasons, the Craft cannot be demonstrated from the pages of a book or internet site. For the most part, it is experiential.

Folk-lore, crafts, superstitions and even basic ritual can be easily laid out, but only by mouth-to-ear, may the subtle nuances be realised. This requires absolute commitment, sadly a virtue that is so very thin on the ground, and unwavering dedication, to oneself, the path and to the Tutelary deities of a Clan or Family. Ancestral spirits readily recognise signs of integrity and strong will; and respond in like manner. No theatre may fool the 'other,' no matter the bafflement of the fool absorbed in illusory acts. Pure mind, speech and heart are essential for spiritual advancement. Fire is the divine sun, and smoke, the divine moon; those who learn this law will pass through the fire that does not burn. Apart from the 'Od' exception (*Odhr*), many of us need a guide through these praxis. Both Roy Bowers and Evan John Jones were 'Od's' men.[7] Bowers knew such apprehension could not be taught or learned, one simply 'got' it, or one did not. At best, it has to be awakened, by ritual initiation.

> "*Since I do not normally have eyes that see, I have to give you others' descriptions of some of the things observed. A woman dressed in white, pacing with us, a skull from the north, and the many others seen by the group. Necromancy? Never, just the opening of the Castle gates, these things appear for a short while only, then the big event begins. One cannot cross the Lethe without some heart-searching and nail-biting. It is hard like this until our guide appears, then we are through.*"[8]

There is so much more than this. True absorption induces a mystical sophistication, a spiritual assurance characterised by the maturity and majesty of prime potencies. We believe whatever we are culturally conditioned to see. Ultimately, we need to remove all self-imposed limitations that impede full concourse with all archaic spirit forms we 'see' generated by those beliefs, be they Elves, Fairies, or demons.

One has to go beyond what can easily be seen. Only then, in solitary thought, are they able to begin the journey into themselves, beyond all bounds of matter. One has to learn to live within this world, in order to excel beyond it. Experience alone leads to knowledge that allows us to comprehend Truth. Experience affords the wisdom to seek humility, to acquire a void of ego. Through this pilgrimage we witness the beauty of the 'gift'. To see life clearly or to remain blind depends always upon individual choice. It is for each of us to learn, that of all the gateways, woman is the most enigmatic. Her role is to first increase all vision, then in full actuality be the very portal of release. In nature it is she who manifests the compassion of Nirvana.

"She [woman] is man's total and absolute equal—and the Goddess's representative upon earth."[9]

Just as masculine qualities associated with God-head suggest the action of 'positive' power, those complementary to them, commonly associated with feminine qualities, may similarly be perceived as the negative kalas of God-head. Woman, is therefore a living image of the wonder of this world in which we live, assuming the role of ferry and destination as one and the same.

"The yarn spell has everything in common with the instinct that makes a mother knit for a forthcoming baby—each stitch is a spell for protection and comfort, wrought by love. Woman is a magical creature, not because of the tides of her

body as Graves suggests, but because she has this power to shape the group entity to her desire and following the tides of her soul she creates magic of no small order in making a home for her offspring. It is the Earth Mother working in her deep instinctive acts and she both creates and influences the group soul. It follows then, in charming, one should follow the tidal movements of the soul, and of the group soul, rather than the intellect and haste of the fiery male. A rhythm worked upon like this strikes a resonance in the group—and power contacts are made. Alchemy and transmutation takes place not because of the material or what is done, but because of the resonance upon the group—and the power of the group. A tide is created, and another tide stilled—a balance wrought."[10]

This is the weight and purpose of the Maid in ritual, she represents the hidden female essence within the holism of absolute sentience, the mirage of the projected world, revealing the hidden divine beyond everything. Ramprasad Sen states that though 'She' is hidden in all things, Her 'self' does not shine out, yet 'She' may be seen by seers, as having superior and subtle intellect.

"It is intent and the love of God in creating the magical substance that transmutes it not any particular power in its own right. The best example of this is woman."[11]

This purity of virtue is evident too within the new born; they are so much closer to the Source. Extrapolated from this, we may realise how the greatest person is the one who has managed throughout their life, even into later years, to keep the heart of a child. Anyone who knew Evan John Jones, or Doreen Valiente, will have seen exactly that: 'Show me your face, the one you had before you were born.' It is the purpose of Mystery Religions to re-organize the misaligned principals that impede our spiritual growth, to re-smelt the individual into gold, to achieve the aim of becoming a raindrop in the ocean, to enable the wonders of the

ANIMA MUNDI

beyond that ignite the soul. The goal of all true magick and religion is not ritual alone, for that is but a simple prop, a tool through which we direct our will towards contact—proof as opposed to basic faith. Those who live for myth and superstition alone are open to frequent deception, and labouring under such restriction, will ultimately lose faith; though often this will be maintained through cajolement or threat. The Underground Stream employs none of these methodologies. Everyone is encouraged to secure their own freedom through genuine personal experiences that bear witness to *the face of the faceless one.*

Within the Clan, candidates are fully supported in their pilgrimages, there to maintain all night vigils in order to experience the sensation of loneliness, loss, and separation from the Clan. Then, in the undertaking of a specific initiation ritual, they are returned into the Clan, to re-join, and continue their own unique and spiritual quest. After all, myths are just a way of explaining how the formless 'other' can be understood; they cannot explain the agonies of the quest, nor the painful stripping away of the self, not even the rapture of revelation, which is not of death, but of life, here, now and beyond. This returns us to the directive:

'You eat this bread in the devils name with girt terror and fearful dread.' [12]

Here alone is stressed the real significance too frequently ignored: *'To thine own end be true.'*

From here we may move onto the importance and relevance of Oaths, a thorny and contentious issue. In the Clan, we all swear individual devotion to our specific Tutelary deity. The purpose in this is dedication, an honouring, an offering and a promise to be 'something', to do 'something', all specific to the Clan. Outside of this personal Covenant with that sentience, we have NO secrets. We all swear to adhere to laws of discretion and respect for our activities and others involved with them. Nothing we do, could ever be considered, 'secret.'

"Any occultist who claims to have secrets is a fake—the only secret is that which man does not understand—otherwise, all wisdom is an open book to those who would read it." [13]

It is often said how, 'There is nothing new under the Sun,' a statement no less true in our current era, and in ancient tome acclaimed. No-one may therefore presume to have the answers that solve and reveal the world's mysteries. The best any may share is their own uniquely individual approach to a perennial truism, and thus the mechanics of their pathway as a specific way to explore and engage those mysteries.

Guidance along a path someone else stumbled upon is key; to 'pay it forward' from one hand to the next, is a gift beyond measure. Anything offered betwixt generation, affords opportunity to follow. Though, always, the individual following that mentor, needs must apply themselves to the tasks given; they alone must complete the actual work for the 'graft' to take hold. Graft, true graft is the symbiosis achieved in this process of application within the 'work—it *is* the work!

Nothing is taken that no-one may give. Evolving technique assists the seeker towards self-realisation of power and purpose. This is the sacred duty of any pilgrim on the path of mysteries. To do less, denudes any office they hold (ie. as in Position of authority as teacher, mentor and priest). Sadly, this will never prevent others claiming otherwise. We must all be wary of those who have little or nothing to share, those who are generally the first to hide behind the cloak of supposed 'secrecy. ' All too quickly do they assert: 'my oath prevents me'… all too much an excuse for having nothing of worth to offer at all. Of course, all quests will always expose the seeker to the guile of confidence tricksters, the undesirable, the insincere, who think to 'steal' what cannot be taken, who think to own what cannot be owned, and who then deign to sell what cannot be sold. Should these acts of barbarism freeze the act of sharing what is essentially, a way of acquiring the knowledge needed, to gain the wit to shift beyond such plaintive spite? We do not believe it should.

The best of us, will always be deceived, and the worst of us will exploit everything. Some protection is in the gift of a group, but not always. Alone with a book and a monitor, what does one really have? Buying into the 'ruse' of secrecy is to inadvertently provide the unscrupulous a shield to hide behind. There is no easy answer. We must take comfort in the fact that what is truly secret is of the divine, and therefore as free as the wind. It is in no man's gift to reveal them. As for discretion, only the honourable will consider fully its worth, the unprincipled will care nothing for its tenets. Whence real knowledge is requested for discussion, it is all too often met by the famous exclamation: 'aaah, secret...' it is worth bearing in mind a response fit to match such falsehood. Yet, if one truly knows their subject, it should be easy enough to explain without giving away unnecessary details as to how things are done exactly, or what is done specifically, or even what is meant literally!

In this way, the genuine may be recognised. As for ourselves, we are happy to admit, we do not know everything, we simply cannot. Life is for learning, and while we live here on this plane of being, we continue to learn. Oaths uphold truth, honour, allegiance and promise to one's Gods, as compacts, therein, and between kindred souls. Glancing casually and randomly through our Craft history confirms that almost every perceived 'secret,' has almost certainly been absorbed, or monopolised by someone else, worked into a book, a lecture, a modality and into praxis too. And yet ... and yet, the Mysteries 'proper,' remain quite undiminished. Beware then, of people who keep grand secrets; trust them not, keep looking, keep searching, for knowledge is freedom and the truth sets all of us free.

> *"No genuine esoteric truth can be written down or put within an intellectual framework of thought. The truths are to be **participated in** during comprehension of the soul."*[14]

Progress, research; push boundaries. Explore, delight in the new, the unexpected; seek always to grow. Discover history, ancestry, the beauty of myth, and the magick of experience. Our past comes alive for us in this way. Roy Bowers stated the most profound of all truths, and so it is worthy of stating again: *"All ritual is prayer."*

All is sacred. Freedom, autonomy and individuality are to be treasured and respected at all times. Welcome all who challenge diverse views and uphold the right of all to exclaim them. Diversity should reveal the dynamic harmony of being, revealing the simplicity of truth and ultimate unity. True debate and freedom of expression explored to the nth degree comes full circle.

Induction and Full Admittance are essential to gain sight of and entrance to the Hearth and Halls of the Mighty Dead, the Mythos, the Mound and Maze and all such Keys to the Stream, awarding the Journeyman recognition and acceptance into the Stream. Though such acts are of incalculable merit, even this does not automatically imbue the surety of 'readiness,' when the time comes. Years of study offer no guarantee; the work is individual and taken in gyfu entirely on individual merit. Privilege is the gift of the 'Other,' and not of any human agent. Therefore, what is scared, remains distinct from secret. Discernment and discretion is requisite. To hold common things as secret is grossly manipulative. Almost certainly, this is why Roy Bowers and Evan John Jones balked against it, believing that too many egotists enforce such moribund tactics, being overly fond of unnecessary power games. The Stream will care for itself, therefore all partakers must be workers in their own right. Passengers simply residing therein, do not automatically qualify for access to any Egregore bound to another, whether that be recent, or of long standing.

Undoubtedly, many are convinced and fervently so, that the longer they 'hold' onto what they assume they 'have,' the more profound and definitive will be their understanding thereof. Suffice to say, this is the same mind-set that asserts how the core of a tradition must never change, nor develop new insights from its practitioners, but must instead remain frozen in time and space as dead words on a page. Indeed, their credo cleaves to stasis; theirs is the 'kiss of death.'

All literature is written as inspired and inspiring texts; yet once recorded, care must be taken to ensure the vitality of the Word must never become atrophied prose, *verbatim in extermino*. For it is the breath alone and not the *word* that carries us forward, the word DOES reveal the lie, but once thought is recorded, it is a dead thing. In hindsight, always deadlier than the sword, but as foresight, viz-à-viz the future, the evolution of that word occurs only if spoken, sung, celebrated anew in the telling. In expiration is it lived and breathed.

Those hoarders of great tomes remain vain fanatics shackled to their testaments of stone—and ever more shall be so. Intent and inference, meaning and significance exist in the message, within the sacred content of the missive; therein lies the Arcanum. Those who seek it in the lines and dots upon a page, seek only decay, a dead thing can never be holy writ. Such is the oxymoron to life, the eternal and divine challenge to the status quo. Therefore to state that no Truth is Secret, is not the same at all as having no 'secrets.' One may reveal truth and excel in the mysteries, but one may conversely choose to follow the lie and hold close its illusory tenets as 'secret.' To maintain a secret, is not to condone the withholding of 'information' as secret; all that may be shared, should be. Everything becomes part of the virtue holder's own lesson, to share and yet to hold, to discriminate and yet to yield, remembering always that:

> *"We are still babies suckling at a breast whose milk is poisonous, yet we think that we flourish upon poison. Truth, no matter how we interpret it, 'feeds demons as well as saints.'"*[15]

Which again is why paper is as dry husk, the grist of in the Mill, stings and scratches; if the narrative is not expressed, nor breathed and given life, the writing withers in the dust. Folktales are indeed replete with regard to the 'Grand Narrative,' of the secret keys, the '*Arcanum glorium*,' the Philosophers Stone no less. How 'cunning' indeed are many artisans of the Craft, who peddle the wares of others, wantonly garnered in the covetous pursuit of the 'Great Work.' In sharing freely all they have learned, they too, will ever be prone to exploitation by others who gain prestige by their labours in turn. And this in spite of the Craft's grand traditions; its own history reveals the devil is not one to reward dishonour, but is ever quick to play adverse trickster, to dance His embrace - 'The Red Death.' Knowledge gained by foul means incurs that same Fate, meted to Faust, et al. Fear of such reprisal once staved the covetous eye at bay, once but no more.

Naturally, gnosis flows for all drawn into its tide. And to those who do explore such streams by tentatively dipping in their toes, or even by full immersion, it is also wise to realise, that in so doing, they have not become the stream; nor likewise its Virtue, nor any part of it, in fact. For it flows unhindered around and over them, moving ever forward—they may sense it, taste, it, smell it, delight in it, or fear its power. Some may gain some experience or even mastery of it, but they will never become it. The Virtue holder/s of the stream alone traverse its course, but always, no matter how meandering that course, will always return to the source— the Ocean.[16]

In one sense, the Virtue holder/s become the stream and therefore determine its nature. How it is held, affects how it flows—or not. If the stream is unnourished, by those who hold Virtue within it, it dries up. Confidence in one's own point of Truth requires no purpose then in engagement, argument or external validation. This is an absolute. Yet, though this may satisfy the virtue holder/s, and even those with whom they work or share it, or those who even recognize it, others, seeking that core purity from afar, may not hear the Truth they cannot see. What we have we hold, but if kept hidden, then no-one sees its light: the Flame of Truth, of Hope and Illumination.

In honouring and protecting the gift of virtue, we need not argue or fight for it. To say what is true and then uphold that in word and deed is sufficient. Of course, those who are able, will see this; though we must remain mindful that those who cannot, would never properly appreciate it, with or without the fight. It is enough to announce the belief in one's own 'truth.' To be silent may appear noble and equally protective of its purity, but may in fact be perceived as a lack of conviction in one's worthiness. As we were taught: ciphers (symbols, sigils, signs and riddles) serve the ego; sound (the paean) serves the soul, and silence serves all spirit. Life demands all three be executed in different measure according to need, and never desire. We do the work, we make our mark, we live, we raise the Guiden Pole for the Pale Lady, under whose aegis we stand. We hold the mound, seeding the ground, resolute, for each generation to follow; and long may it be so.

To grasp with a lateral mind the subconscious subtleties and nuances of pleromic fusion as an essential enigma, and to accept without prejudice, mysteries yielded and/or experienced in that process (analogies to smithcraft notwithstanding), generates an extant ability to evolve comprehension through apprehension. A lack here indicates a perception falling outside that realm. It's about moving beyond conscious boundaries, quite literally, as an achievable epiphanic inductive process of illumination. Be ever mindful that in seeking 'power,' the only thing invoked is the refined edge of virtue, and not its core. Within the latter, that 'power' takes the form of the dragon as the Ouroboros, consumed by autophagia. In the former, the dragon is transmuted by 'virtue' of its fire. Truly, we begin to understand this beautiful wisdom in the context of the Clan Mythos, where, through the medium-ship of Sophia, the King re-gains his crown.

2
A
Basic structure
of the Craft

"The efficacy of religion lies precisely in what is not rational, philosophic or eternal; its efficacy lies in the unforeseen, the miraculous, the extraordinary. Thus religion attracts more devotion according as it demands more faith,—that is to say, as it becomes more incredible to the profane mind. The philosopher aspires to explain away all mysteries, to dissolve them into light. Mystery on the other hand is demanded and pursued by the religious instinct; mystery constitutes the essence of worship, the power of proselytism." [17]

Religion and/or belief is a marker for our Faith. Through it, many inadvertently generate the means of self-imprisonment and myopia. We may thusly be judged as beings who forge their own chains; likewise, we each have the ability and choice to liberate that 'self.' In freeing ourselves from all perceived obstructions to the 'Work,' we are free from its encircling fear within. Yet, that deceives through its pretences of quasi-support within proximity; in reality, it is merely suffocation. This illustrates the gaoler and the liberator and the many levels of chains that bind, from those imaginary, to the liminal; and to those forged of physicality.

The temple of the Shekinah is likewise the self, in communion through all such media. It rises within as a symbol beyond all forms of interpretation. For many years, theologians have asserted the favourable belief that animism is the greater and more sophisticated of all comprehensions. Animism speaks to the soul on all levels, where Monotheism fails utterly. Panentheism yields the realisation that everything is simply not inhabited by god but IS within god—IS god in fact. Perhaps the best way to learn anything, including how to understand a thing, is to *stand under* it. There, taken apart and turned over, we are returned; albeit with insights from beyond: that is, with *kenning*. This is perhaps why the gnostic is akin to the Brahmin, who once insisted all devotional acts transpire in natural environs. Knowing, brings true liberation. Many things will always appeal and seduce the mind, yet where we chose to engage these matters directly, in their embrace, the soul is given true solace.

> *"The student of the 'Mysteries' is essentially a searcher after Truth, or as the ancient traditions called it—Wisdom."*[18]

The Mysteries, properly described, are that precise resonance distinguishable as gifts of 'divine' communication, rather than expressions of divination accessed by exoteric means. Those artes, presented within a framework of spirituality and communion with the 'Other,' in all its forms of mediation, emanate from the ethereal realms through all vital links that earth such principles into realisation.

Divination has held an honoured and very sacred purpose among all ancient mystery religions, an aspect much overlooked in our modern age, and with considerable regret. Robert Cochrane (aka Roy Bowers) referred to these artes, stressing the imperatives of poetic and mythic visioning as true keys of the Seer. Traditional heathen culture, natural to the progressive flux of peoples migrating to these sacred isles, is a most worthy arte. Understanding the historical role of Seiðr and giving it expression in our modern age, is a duty to culture we fully support. We bear witness to parallel principles inherent of that culture as a Faith to live by.

Yet somewhere in the medieval flux, the best and worst extremes developed into a culture that was broad enough to encompass the most profound and deeply magical principles of Faith, and by contrast, a Faith that was so encompassing, life and culture were anathema to it. Fundamental to both examples are the natural traces of Gnosticism, in the purest cosmological sense. These deserve some detailed exploration, especially as they are all pertinent to the writings and beliefs of Roy Bowers, whose Faith was broad enough to glean the gems of tradition, set within the starry tiara of the ineffable heavens—time and tide; fate and duty. We each mark them as we are moved to do so, according to the measure of culture within the Faith adhered to, and the quality of Faith within that culture, as it is lived and breathed, each and every day. In the **Structure of the Craft** document (ii), Bowers' also remarks with full conviction how:

> *"From the Gods came seven children, who created seven worlds to rule over, and they form a halo about the Great Gods as seven stars."*

He continues, describing the forms and landscapes that manifest elements through all creation under the aegis of four of those seven Gods. The rest of that section of the letter concerns the description of the Castles that guard those four lands, and the Gods who rule them. In another chapter of this book, the similarities of this cosmogony to a gnostic creation myth is discussed in lieu of the role of Fate and the divine feminine—'Truth' then, as the upholder of all Law and Justice, Mercy and Severity, Compassion and Judgment, Love and Ambivalence, the 'real' force of civilization and evolution. In fact, there is a folkloric legend that attributes the knowledge of Tubal Cain as the gift of his sister, the beautiful Na-maah. Just as Oðin received his from Freyja, and Loki from Angrboða. In the eddic poem '*Baldrs draumar,*' Oðin requires the prophesy of the Vølur summoned as spirit from Hela's realm. He says to her:

"No wise-woman art thou, nor wisdom hast;
Of giants three, the mother art thou."

Some have suggested this might refer to *Angrboða* as 'Mother' of three monsters. This mighty Jotun states that she will never more be charmed from those realms again until Loki is again loosed from his bonds. For she is—*Iárnvidjur* the true Wood-Wose, the dryadic wraith of the Ironwood—*Iárnvidia*, the great and mighty forests grown gnarled upon the rich blood acres of ancestral mounds, of the dead and the Mighty Dead together in their tombs of stone, from an aeon ago, when man walked with his gods.

In fact, as the seven 'kalas' those starry rays, of light and wind, are the manifest force within the Seven Rishis, the divinely inspired genius of the ante-deluvian priests to the wisest of monarchs, and who were later perceived also as the archangels of Judaeo-Christian theology. Yet these seven Assyrian beings were winds, and yet were equally chthonic, of the earth, sky and sea—no fire, as fire alone is Promethean. It is Lucifer's Crown, the diadem of Holy Gnosis, the sacred inspiration of the One Creatrix. He is the 'light and fire' from Her dark and murky depths, the 'watery' Apsu, the depths, of Pluto, the treasures within— of Himself, the dragon, the Revealer, the keeper of Hades and the rim of Hel, where he escorts us hence across the wasteland to the Chinvat bridge of Heavenly realm.

"Prayer is the breathing in and out the one breath of the universe"[19]

Moreover, those 'seven' virtues emanate from the Ultimate Godhead as divinely feminine forces radiated through all perceptions we may hold of Her, to condense as manifest form, the masculine virtues we attribute to all His many faces and masks. They are together, each light and shade to the other, water and air, fuelled by fire. As they do not therefore contain or reflect that light, they are the shadows cast by it, yet they 'carry' its potential, again infused as the dark seed within, the inspiration to know—the true message. Just as the winds and the kalas that flow from the stars and all celestial bodies are invisible, with the exception of the divine triad of the Sun, Moon and Venus, their 'virtue' is immensely influential. They are the 'messengers' in this sense. Yet their lustre is known only by the light in whose shade they are cast. Christian theology states that no angel shines by their own light as they are but reflections of the one 'true light.'

As a view, this very probably obfuscates the fact that theology likewise asserts its belief that angels have no soul, therefore no fire (fire = soul in orthodox Christian theology); without fire, they may never shine independently. The Moon reflects back only light that falls upon its face. It is dark where shadows cast it, forever emanating the 'hidden' attributes of itself, rather than the visible reflections of the glorious Sun. As each archangel is regent to a planet, therefore reflecting the light of the Sun, they are also transposers of the virtue of that Planet, invisibly. Therefore, we have named them 'Shadows of God—'Mal'akh.' Malkah, also means Queen (but pertains to diverse interpretation dependent upon contextual qualification). This is not a variant of the better known spellings found in 'melech' or 'malekh' signifying angel or king respectively, but the etymological root of both, in its original feminine form.[20] Herself, then as 'darkest' Night. Malkah = Queen. The seven teaching and civilising artes as primal forces, and as spheres of knowledge in terms of the Craft of life, the gifts of the sages or Apkallu appear in Hindu religion as Saptarishis also.

"The darkness of the Mind [exists] that we may reach the uncreated light, to find union we need to strip away all images and pre-conceptions."

Albertus Magnus (1200-80) a 13th century Dominican theologian and tutor to Thomas Aquinas, asserted the above observation. A few hundred years later, another mystic, Angelus Silesius added:

"Who in this mortal life, would see the light, that is beyond all light, beholds it best by faring forth, into the darkness of the Night."

Given that the *Apkallu* (teaching spirits and divine ancestors) of Mesopotamian lore are also equated with the Wind, it is useful to consider another line in Roy Bowers' 'Basic Structure' where he describes to us how:

"Above the head of the Moon, as shewn [sic] in the diagram lies five (seven) other stars, known as the Goddesses, that is they are to be seen in The Plough or Haywain." [21]

An astute observer has suggested this glyph, is probably a graphic expressed of the Seal of Solomon where the:

*"The Four Winds being the foundation of each triangular formation with two of the three being expressed in the Apex of each triangle. As they descend and rise to "meet" the apex points become 'one' —Four foundational winds and one that is experienced as three (or at three different stages of being). Perhaps found poetically and artistically proposes the Swastika as the four fiery winds and the Gankyil as the three turning*s"[22]

This is remarkably insightful as the triskele upon the qutub as the drive shaft for the four Cardinal winds/wheels of virtue (swastika) that cumulatively serve as a succinct sigilised image of the Merkavah. A fine example of the myriad designs this movement evokes. As ruler of the Winds, the *'Windyat'* [23] is a force of considerable enigmatic speculation. Roy Bowers' intent in this passage, developed from old Germanic and Gothic language roots, reflect his increasing passion for discovery within a his own instinctive sense of roots, in a culture of blood and bone, of his fore-fathers, one he could sense in mind and body, one that sang to his soul. The first sense of this is found in the use of a pole the (qutub), as 'whip' to the wind; the second implies a 'winnowing' of being threshed, thrown about, ground in the (wind) Mill itself. It brings to mind the beautiful and evocative poem by Gibran in which he says:

"Like the sheaves of corn he gathers you unto himself.
He threshes you to make you naked.
He sifts you to free you from your husks.
He grinds you to whiteness.
He kneads you until you are pliant;
And then he assigns you to his sacred fire,
that you may become sacred bread for God's sacred feast."

In consulting the etymology of whip, (Windyat) we discover that it is rooted in the meaning indicating swift movement, a nod perhaps to the hermaphroditic forms of 'Mercury,' and 'Hermes,' apropos to Tettens; Keepers and Guardians all, specifically of the Mound—the Ancestral mound, of the Mighty Dead. How then to loosen the quick to cross the Lethe and be among the dead, for... *"the witch crosses the river, the pagan stays with the quick."*

♦ **Feast and Famine**

"If the brain and body are burning clean with fasting, every moment anew, song comes out of the fire...be empty...write secrets...Fasting is Solomon's ring; don't give it to some illusion and lose your power."[24]

In a letter to Bill Gray,[25] Roy Bowers instructs him with regard to the preparatory approach to ritual; that is to say, how we focus attention through acts of discipline mostly centred upon 'fasting' before the 'knots.' Not everyone marks the knots with such abstinence, deeming it unnecessary in modern occult praxes. Certainly, we have found that fasting weakens the body, so that shaking free of it, is far easier. There are other considerations for and against this demonstration of ritual discipline. There is no substitute for a correct and sensible controlled fast (with the caveat that no extreme of asceticism is necessary).

We 'travel' further and faster on a light stomach, therefore, as a discipline, it must be precisely honed in order to conquer the demands and discomforts of the body's whims (rather that its needs). Manual work requires a greater calorific intake than sedentary occupations. The purpose is not to become an emaciated ascetic, but to balance the right amount needed to function without recourse to excess. This inculcates the basic surrender of all personal passion or attachment to the form and force hostile to deep experiential gnosis. This is why Roy Bowers advocated that all things be actuated, in truth, and at all times.

Prior to any rite, we do fast, cutting out all meat, (additional) salt, chocolate, caffeine, alcohol and processed foodstuffs for seven days prior to a working, becoming increasingly aware of the subtle changes in our body chemistry, our moods and our awareness/alertness. Afterwards, a well-earthed body from which the 'en-lightened' spirit is decreasingly attached, serves well to properly ground and balance the body, restoring it once again to a focused state of normal operation for that individual. On the day of the rite itself, water, fruit and juice only may be consumed (with the exception of those on medication), who require snacks to accompany them and ease the toll on their digestive systems.

The 'Work,' as a serious alchemical construct, processes the disintegration and re-absorption/integration throughout its peripatetic actuations. 'Houzle' is the Saxon expression for the meaning and significance of the communal cup or horn shared in companie. As part of the sacred feast following a holy rite, it has been described by some as a version of the Eucharist. Consisting simply of bread, wine and salt, with seldom variation, a distinct conglomeration of spirit imparted during its sacramental realization, becomes 'essentially' drawn into all celebrants. More than a celebration, it forms an integral conclusion to any rite whilst reducing further risk of residual hunger. All share in the high honour expiated through full and active participation. Having no bearing of gluttony or any other similar negative excess, a true feast varies enormously due to the nature, season and significance of the rite.

Indulgence is hardly ever going to provide a valid charge against noted efficacy. In examples from the ecclesiastical Calendar, we may freely note the expression: 'giving it up for lent.' This is the basic surrender of a personal passion or attachment to the form and force hostile to deep experiential gnosis. This is again, why Roy Bowers insisted upon the self, holding true to itself, at all times. If we lose that, we lose the intrinsic reality of the Eucharistic juncture. Everyone present for the rite partakes of both Houzle and feast. Resolute in many traditions, is the additional belief that sacred foods offered through the Houzle, should include certain entheogens as effective elements to enable the persons partaking of them, to move (faster, though not necessarily deeper, nor more coherently) beyond the worlds, thereto work magick aided by forces manifest. But, more frequently, due to their vital nature, these are eaten during a given rite where they properly fulfil their essential purpose, rather than at its conclusion.[26] The carrier itself becomes important as a vehicle for the transmission of those entheogens. Hence, various plant extracts, steeped and distilled into wine tinctures and tisanes, fully absorb the requisite elements as aides in the otherworld 'journey;' the alcoholic base is far more effective than grape or fruit juice.

Careful understanding must be employed in choosing the base substances, as all variants considered, require mythic qualification. Indeed

Bowers warns Gills[27] of their potencies, of unknown qualities and of unpredictability, noting the grinding emphasis upon the gravid risks undertaken in their consumption. Imbibement of entheogens become the very bread and/or wine as rapid transvectors for something greater or deeper, and must always be considered as the supreme imperative of that purposeful instruction, rather than indulged for the effects borne of its own sake. If for example, one is considering the base elements of fruit and wheat as elements of the natural landscape imbibed, then such may easily be fashioned and transmitted without further processing as alcohol or preserves. Wine and mead are naturally partaken within many traditions. Considered as the gift of the gods, they are shared to express their liberating and euphoric virtues, rather than basic qualities of fluid

GUNDUSTRUP CAULDRON

viscosity. For others choosing not to imbibe alcohol and other historical substances, etc, then fruit juice must suffice to mark at least the gestural quality of this exchange. In all examples, the produce consumed must remain with the individuals concerned, and agreed upon within the bounds of their natural traditions.

Partake of bread, as the staff of life, wine, drawing upon divine life-blood through all produce of the sacred vine and salt, raw gift of life, as Manna borne of earth. In their sacred consumption, each participant observes the triune grace of the Three Mothers in salt (earth); bread (air) and wine (water/blood). Collectively, in their gift, a well-balanced Houzle is essential to communal experience and understanding, revealing how the subtle bodies interact and fulfil our spiritual aspirations.

Feasting secures typical completion of all rites, satisfying the sensory deprivations exerted upon the body prior to that rite, grounding its magicks within temporality. Even in that course of action, dependent upon the meat consumed, the body may find itself flooded with an endorphin rush generated by sensory saturation, inducing yet another level of euphoria subsequent to the rite itself. Always choose organic, seasonal foodstuffs, unprocessed, and try, where possible to cook them as simply as possible. When they hit the belly, their impact will be immediate, with pork especially. Observing noted archaic proscriptions most carefully, feasting should properly honour the assigned meat through 'taboo' whence imposed: absorbing the essence of one's Tutelary deity through consumption of a beast associated with that deity or ancestral totem, is Eucharist indeed. Many view such an act as rank heresy, a heinous blasphemy, held in contempt and fear. Conversely, certain sensitivities demand the breaking of perceived 'taboo;' therefore, some might rightly question the veracity of a truly sacred Eucharist. To answer this to the satisfaction of the individual, we need to explore the virtue and purpose of taboo. Yet consuming the shared body and blood within established constructs and within specific contexts, whilst holding conducive perception, allows for transcendence that draws immanence in its strengthening of group bonds and identity. Without such requisites, tis naught but vanity, a blasphemy even; but if one consumes their sacrament, with reverence and humility, with both fear and love of the god that flesh represents, then there is no finer celebration of 'god-eating.'

All things should and must be considered and questioned to ensure accord with each person's *geis*, most specifically as individual pilgrims in their own search for the grail. Thus, by making the outer circle of salt, we consecrate our efforts to the Godhead. Any authoritative 'body' worth its salt,[28] should be able to demonstrate the means and reasons for its 'Laws,' principally those that refer to taboo. They should never simply 'be,' but must have clear and acceptable, though not necessarily fully 'realised' causality and consequence. All Laws, where they exist within those eminent 'bodies' of authority, once filtered through that process of analysis, should thereafter find peaceful acceptance upon Admission to them, but never without such aforementioned scrutiny. Where conflict exists, no vow or oath is advisable. Once given; it should remain infrangible.

"Law—this has now become his credo:
Do not what you desire—do what is necessary.
Take all you are given—give all of yourself.
What I have I hold.
When all else is lost—and not until then.
Prepare to die with dignity"[29]

As stated, taboo and *geis* exist to impart the Mystery and Truth of Godhead. Blasphemy exists in certain traditions and religions where knowledge of that mystery is not respected or honoured. Whence democracy be desirable within a Clan family, in actuality, it presents a neglectful obstruction to the duties and service given to the People by their sworn Head-kinsmen. If there is no Trust to be intuited within them, and the Laws appear oppressive and unjust, then the individual seeker must surely look elsewhere for Companie along the lonely road. Faith in the Mythos should be absolute, Trust in one's Kinsmen should be absolute; in neither case should these be cold or blind, but won in the Ring of Souls, the domain of Beauty in Truth. This introduces the nature of the 'Wican Rede' in relation to The Law. Some posit they are similar enough to have a shared origin that expresses primarily the principle of free will, of Choice, whereas, I would posit that The Law rather suggests we really don't have free will at all. Not in the final solution. Whatever we do affects everything, and in all cases, change occurs, as it must. But, need compels us to act, desire affords the latitude of an illusion of choice. A mere mainstay. '*An it harm none?*' An oxymoron, surely? The fallout either way will always harm someone, it is naive to think otherwise.

The Rede is clever, for in suggesting the option of choice, we must realise we have none in this reality. For our will is born of desire. True will is acting without recourse to desire or need. Hence we realise we have no choice. Fate is all we face in life, and believing or assuming it to be a 'battle,' especially one we can defeat, we fail already. Overcoming Fate, means to stop the wheel, to cease the endless round, the march of time. Defeating Fate requires a surrender to its flow, and not to lose oneself in needless battle. To hold fast to the self, the need, that is ultimately the requisite to overcome, to know and retain the self within eternity, and if we fail, then we must bow to the superior kenning of Fate and begin again. This is neither fatalistic, which accepts that things cannot be changed, nor is it deterministic, as nothing can be determined as each action induces counter reaction for every choice we believe we make in earnest. Destiny is the grail, and the only oblique Choice we truly have, is whether or not to accept that to achieve it, is conversely not to conform to either extreme. Perception is everything. Belief is nothing. Choice is an illusion. Riding the eye of the storm is a matter of kenning. It is neither need nor desire. The Rede and The Law meet only in their rejection of illusion.

♦ Riddle Reason and Rhyme

The handmaiden of death am I
A sister to the scourge
A slow breaker of men.
My arms have raised up rebels, saints and gods
and held them to my chest as they died.
Yet emptied of my burden I offer up hope.
Kings have knelt before me in fear and wonder.
I have been kissed by Queens
Propositioned by clergy
And spat upon by doomed knights.
Demons fear my gaze.

Does this suggest 'Fate,' the Moon, or something else entirely? As a fascinating riddle, it is redolent of the famous kennings of the Exeter Book, yet reads equally well for the Tao. Pondering upon all Handmaidens of Fate, we encounter the Valkyries of Norse myth, not as warriors, for their gift is greater still; even to the gods. Alongside humankind, myth affords even the gods spiritual salvation, a form of redemption; all in the gift of the 'Handmaidens of Fate.' This vigour compels the natural, cyclical law of destruction, redemption and creation. Redemption is not here deemed in any remote way, similar to biblical transgression, but is better expressed as a restoration of a former order, albeit one reformed in gnosis; ergo, one now removed from errant decision, of failure to make the mark. Wise through experience; it now seeks opportunities to add evolutionary positivism to the consanguinity betwixt man and god.

Time is again, the manifest and absolute constant within this formula. In surrender, we display our triumph over all unnecessary or superfluous attachments to things allied to corporeality. Borne of an understanding that transports us through our devotions, the oath is irrevocable to the 'þing,' and to the unfurling of the realised self, especially within that deific and ancestral environment. As an area of protected ground, '*þorn*'- the *þing* becomes the holy space where each pledge their duty to The Law and to Wyrd. In that sacred ring we make our shift to see the gods, to know them and transcend only those aspects deemed as impedances to our own growth, and of leisure too in being and becoming who we are and will be, Earthly existence, preserves and honours always, the beauty and vitality of its purpose, and the virtue of its truths. In one of his letters to Joe Wilson during the last few months of his life, Bowers recalls giving instructions in Companie that very strongly invoke the 'Three Mothers' within the making and weaving of the cord as Fate. One might even allude to the Kabbalah in the assignation of blue/black with *mem*— water, red with *shin*—fire and white with *aleph*—air/spirit.

> *"Flax is a common cultivated flower known as Linum. The variety known as Narbonense is very good—it is also a decorative in a garden. It is gathered and hung to semi-dry in darkness. When it is nearly dry beat it with a mallet made of wood until the fibres are separated from the stem. This produces a linen 'shoddy.'*

> *These are combed out with a teazle head until they are reasonably separate, then spun upon a distaff by a woman who 'sings' to the moon (sounds crazy?) This linen shoddy should be dyed before combing or spinning by Alder bark for red, blackberries (or equivalent) for blue, and bleached in lime or chalk for the white.*

41

Your whole length should be measured in this, then seven knots tied in the plait—and then you have the beginnings of a cord which is worn about the waist or neck and used as a meditational device, a la 1734. The remains should be kept in the separate colours and spun upon the distaff. This, used with Mother Broom, and symbolic herbs, will assist the cure of most illnesses if a piece is tied and charmed around the afflicted part and three knots tied. I know it sounds crazy but—from personal experience I know it works. I have seen the common cold cured, cancer of the womb, warts, and bleeding stopped by this yarn—but it is dependent upon the moon's phases, and Mother Broom for the inner workings. The slow process of creating the yarn is a form of alchemy. If your wife uses it, she must not use the Alder, but instead turn to blackthorn for a black thread, but be careful of that yarn for it carries the power to blast."[30]

The woven 'knot' is therefore perfectly suited in purpose as the emblem of Inanna atop her reed pillar forming a somewhat idiosyncratic 'ankh' also a symbol for the Virtue of life. Coincidentally, this binding of the elements within a sacred enclosure is denoted by the graphic for salt, earth and the gateway known as Malkuth in the Kabbalah. Magically, it represents the circle of arte and by reflux; some occultists perceive it as 'Daath' the Gateway to the Supernal realms. Hekate is the three-fold gateway to Heaven, Earth and the Underworld, leading into the fourth realm of enlightenment; beyond Time. Placed in the Halls of the Gods, the poetic Castle, Time, resides spiritually in Ceugent.

'Hael to the Mothers Three!'

♦ Mask and Stang

"We work with the three pronged stave or 'stang' "[31]

The devil's trident, the fool's baton, the hayfork is the ubiquitous staff of the ardent crafter, masked only by intent where all ritual is prayer; all work is grist. We raise the Stang for Dame Fate and for He who manifests

Her causality, Ol' Tubal, Master Artificer and Craftsman, the Sabbat King and Hooded Wanderer. In all guises, this is known. All things interact at a soul level, without exclusive transfer between humans, and to other forms, extending also to animals; in fact, all flora and fauna. Compelled quite unanimously towards certain people, animal forms and symbolic identity, we all share a collective sentience, albeit filtered within each of us along the way. Hence we must choose carefully what we say and to whom it is said; whom we may 'work' with, how we may present our many faces, and to whom we share it.

One media alone affords us impunity from such caution. Lacking in all such personal inflection or assistant intonation, the written word may quickly convey unwarranted false impression, just as physical proximity may deceive intent. Coupled with a natural propensity towards personal bias, individual research develops intuitive faculties, reacting instinctively to relevant mystical texts. Contra to vain subtleties, that one 'other' media excels in its impactful processing, serving well in its visual ability to communicate: the *Mask*.

Masks help us to recognise, distinguish, disguise, generate fear, create security, change character, adopt persona, align a philosophy, and to bring a wave of superstition to men of science! Much depends upon the wearer, and upon purpose, finding expression through the medium of the mask itself to empower or conceal! Designed to 'host' ancestral power, some physical proponents of the mask appear intuitively separate from all that remains 'unseen.' Consideration for their construction might include an understanding of where the mask resides, where the mask ends and the wearer begins, which requires arte to behold us as we cross that liminality. Both Bowers and Jones endorsed and explored their work through masked rites.[32] Once the host relationship between spirit and mind deepens, all boundaries begin to dissolve, and through that shift, transforms the wearer. Thus I say:

"Many are the masks of Man.
Obtuse are guise, trickery and guile.
False are all things visible to Man.
Latent virtue marks the True.
Choice resides within Man.
Agenda determines the mandate.
Predilection resides beyond Man.
Disconnection creates antipathy.
Many are the Masks of God."

A mask is therefore probably one of the most powerful things encountered as a 'tool of arte.' Where engaged with purpose, it has the inherent ability to mediate a given 'stream' of virtue. For the mask to serve as the face of the gods, our totems, or to mediate spirit, et al, it must transpose such via a filter of singular virtue, honour, and truth— otherwise the mask is a hollow dead thing, remaining stagnant, and poisonous. Adornment presents unique Mysteries, explored through the media of their making, serving to facilitate the cross-roads manifesting all form. As Janus looks fore and aft, an astute and insightful expression of the 'Mask' may thus be adopted to both conceal the lie and reveal the truth, yet this paradox presents a virtue pure on either side.

Looking briefly into the etymology of 'Guising,' the masking of the physical form, renders visible the metaphysical mask—the symbiant 'other.' Taken to reflect a change in appearance, most often with intent to deceive, the attached custom of 'guising'[33] is mannered deception by inversion. This often takes on the form of being 'out of dress,' that is to wear one's clothes inside out, upside down, or those of the opposite sex.

From this, there exists the cockney slang term, of 'geezer,' also known as a 'mummer.'

"The fool is by no means a fool, but very much the simple god."[34]

There is much wisdom in the naiveté of the Fool, but also in the Sage who plays one. Though an 'old friend to many,' each new seeker or 'fool' has much to teach us; the 'blind needfully lead the blind. Perhaps the fool is simply blind because his eyes do not yet 'see,' and perhaps we are 'blind,' because in seeing so much, we are often oblivious to peripheral activity - that is, we look but do not truly 'see.' Therefore, we welcome all insights into these amazing tools that can teach us so much about the subconscious and the thresholds of 'Mind.'

The wise holy fool—the alpha omega zero point paradox, neither the end nor the beginning, androgynous hermaphrodite who is all, and nothing. The 'simpleton,' who is yet all knowing; pregnant with potential for renewal, yet desiring it not, seeks freely, openly, guided ever from within, not distracted from without; The self, qutub, connected to the Source, inflamed with divine vigour, enfolded by the wings of Fate, this fool dances on.

Written into our Clan Cosmology is the directive to work under the stars within a ring of stones, hedged by trees and by a river if possible. There to feel the burning sting of the wind upon one's skin, be awed by the grand vista of stars and to draw orgone from all those subtle elements that surround us; shared with brethren in Companie, it is unmatchable by any other craft of man. There can be no finer temple than this; it is our world, the seat of Himself en-souled by Her, a fountain of earthly delights. Imagine then a T-shaped cross, hewn from the trunk of a living oak left to rot in the place of sacrifice. As our mentor rightly said, no longer is it considered necessary that anyone or anything should give their life to mark the particular rite that acknowledges the original 'sacrifice' of the gods that we might have life. Instead, a sickle is placed at the foot of the Clan Stang to invoke this archaic practice, symbolically recreating the Mythos of the dying man/god on the Tau cross.[35]

Preferably absent of any garland, the Stang signifies the memory of that sacrificial death. It is accompanied by skull, crossbones, knife & cup. In death, we must all face the Grim Reaper. Yet, we believe there is so much more to death than just dying. The Mask is best defined by an appropriate tool to mark the tide, rather than flora (belonging to, and of the gods already), serving as testament to our craft and wit of application. True gyfu. Our souls survive death and shift into rebirth many times, we mindfully work towards its release through cumulative gnosis attaining spiritual unity with the Godhead. Here we see the Stang as an altar standing in the forecourt of an open tomb or burial. Because the Old God was, in essence, considered to be Lord of manifest things in all their forms, this made perfect sense. The Totem, the Clan leader and the God shared the same essence and were symbolically of the same 'family.' Hence we say:

"The Hunter, the Hunted (Old Tubal Cain) and the Roebuck in the Thicket are one and the same."

Bones serve as a graphic reminder of our fragile mortality, and of the blood and dust from which we are formed. Stripped to this primal image, we gaze into the 'mask' of the Pale-Faced Goddess. At the appointed time she comes as the Immortal Beloved with her kiss of death. Looking further still into the Mythos of the staff and the Stang, and onwards to their origins in the Asherah pole, we come to their use as tools to aid in prophetic and oracular praxes. Words are formed of letters accrued with symbolic intent—potent sigils if you will. From the Phoenician letter *Pe* we acquire the Greek symbol 'Pi', with both representing 'gate.' Stylistically, they differ a little though, and again they each lend something to a runic symbol and primal letter *Yr*, which forms the root of W*yrd*hr and U*rd*hr. There is also another rune that represents the oracular or divinely prophetic 'mouth,' Os. From a schematic point of view, Yr more closely resembles Pi in imagery than Os; but again, there is greater complexity still, when we consider the rune 'P' itself. Phonetically, it is cognate with Pe/Pi and has the additional correlation to oracular 'opening' in the sense of Wyrdhr. That rune is Peorthro— the inspiring cauldron, the font and well of wisdom, of memory and the measure of our Fate. It reflects action upon mind.

> "*As far as we can see, it has two effects. One is the activating of the power in a human body, and the other is moving the centre of power from one point, to another [...] It evidently affects the nerve and mind power that has its centre just over the front of the head [...] now from what we gather, when you move* **the cleft stick** *down, it also affects the other centres on the body, such as the one just under the heart and above the sexual organs. In other words, it is a far more advanced method than that used by the ceremonial magicians who do all this by breathing.*" [36]

The above remark made to Norman Gills by Roy Bowers, regards the use of the 'cleft' stick,[37] and how the pressure and application of its use onto the body, achieves a shift of personal virtue throughout it. Following on from that, we may note the relative comments used by Bowers to describe the 'assumption of the mask,' where that same, personal virtue, is consciously invoked, prior to any rite or working.

> "*The Blessing. This is made before the altar Stang, no lights. The form of self-blessing should be used as per 'mask'. It is also the assumption of the magical personality. Major key is used by initiates.*"[38]

What Bowers alludes to is the circulatory vibrations, in sympathetic tune (now akin to bio-rhythms) to the tidal flux coursing around the body, through the veins, flooding finally into the brain, to entrance and induce the thunderous rupture of '*Seiðr.*' Bowers hints further of this to Gray where his disdain for the formality of the Kabbalah is clarified in his statement regarding its three pillars as culturally 'alien,' to his Craft and that he used instead '*an anthropomorphic pattern to shift virtue*' upwards from the ground to the heavens. Moreover, he considered his 'Faith' to be basically 'feminine,' making cryptic comments about the altar as the '*godstone.*' [39]

Bowers embraced folklore and folk magicks as a ravenous wolf at dinner. Overwhelmed by the profound and extraordinary expression of the works shared with him by the '*Old man of Westmoreland,*' he wrapped his own knowledge around them, producing quite exceptional gateways through into the Mound and to the Castles of the Kingly realms. One of those engages the combination of the broom and sword and of two brooms also. Staves, in all forms, stunted, carved, bent, twisted, set into tools or simply 'masked,' have always signified the sacristy of the three mysteries, male, female and priestly. Where the Cuveen Stang is placed centrally within the working area emulating the axial pole, geomantic Omphalos of the universe, the Paracelsion character of chthonic theory or forces of the '*Stang and Serpent*' are said to open this ring. When placed to the South (Earth), squaring the circle with the staves of the elements, the '*Broom and Lamp*' form the bridge that fords the magickal tides of manifest causes.

This quaking within and without, reflects the virtue of Thunr who has arcane cognates in Baal-Peorm known as 'Lord of the Cleft.' [40] Typically, cleft being an opening, infers the mouth, meaning Baal-Peorm is an utterer, a speaker, a master of the Word, for wit and wisdom, genius and deceit. Likewise, in sharing the root *Pe* Thunr shares similar virtue to Hadad, and his more arcane counterpart, Rimmon, Earth-shakers and Thunderors, all. At a holy site (Baal-Bek) dedicated to this thunderous deity, Baal, there is a quivering gate named Ba-Bel, to his sacred Temple, upon the mound that inspires prophecy and oracular wisdoms induced as inspired utterances. As a phallic fertility god of storm, Baal, is there depicted as two large stones aside a palm tree, emphasising the 'cleft' of Asherah.

Inspiration is ever the domain of the divine feminine, and always She is central to all other things that may flank Her as pillars, or surround her as within a Grove. She is the pole, and the 'rider' mounts her in vision to see beyond what mortal eye may witness. Wisdom has always nestled within the skull-cap, the favoured cup of grace. Sutures within the skull open, creating a 'cleft' betwixt them for the spirits to rise and meld within the ethereal forms of the 'other.' Homer records the myth of Athena's birth from the '*Karenon*,' a word describing both a mountain peak and the head. Zeus births Athena form his *clefted* cranium; the literal crown, the glorious virtue of wisdom itself, the Word, in all three forms of Beauty, of (pure) Love, and of Truth itself. Pythia straddles the cleft of Delphi, whence Apollo rises as wisdom's heir, breathing oracle and prophecy. Medusa, likewise, spawns Her serpents. Radiant aureoles form to witness the enhancement of virtue, a true shining, emanating forth, beaming from the ruptures, the cleft of partition, the space 'in-between.'

Typically, Ishtar is another earlier form of this wisdom goddess. She rules creation from the Kur, meaning the (netherworld) mountain plundered in Her lust for the triple Crown (Koryphe—rulership by right of the Mé). These combined myths share enough to suggest confusion has arisen, possibly due to numerous translations that cloud our understanding of the symbology and significance of the crown, the head and cleft relative to the birth and to actuation of divine wisdom 'rising' as supreme personage. Her 'thunder' is that of the *Seiðr*. Again, SHE is the Tree of Wisdom, and of life and death.

Commonly referred to in folkloric terms, *'The Talking Stick'* (not the baton held to impugn unwarranted speech), is designed to stand betwixt the ground and the fore-head/ perineum, so that when leaned upon, we may be said to be sorely pressed, or within the 'cleft' of the Oracle Herself. Prosaic application, noted by the metaphorical axiom: *'when we are between a rock and a hard place,'* refers to the remarkable capacity we have for the acquisition of insight and intuition acquired when stimulated by external pressure.[41] In the simplest of objects, is the most obscure and profound where 'import' is always 'hidden within plain sight.' The image given is of a stick, partially severed along the grain of the wood to make a springy clasp for some object, often a candle. Anything held in this way is in an unyielding embrace, unable to move, from which the figurative expression derives. This device is exactly that described by Bowers in the same letter, where he discusses the addition to the *cleft stick* made of ash, of a particular balanoid fossil.[42] Similar to the Greek Thyrsus, this acorn shaped wand would generate a process he describes as: 'balanite & ash'.[43] This was sometimes used in conjunction with the Cat's Cradle (a descriptor for a harness and a positional mandala for the actual rite) and sometimes smeared with an unguent to increase and accelerate this stimulating process. When discussing this with E.J.J, he stated the term covered all usages and Bowers was using his typical fondness for 'grey magic' upon Gills to test him for his responses.

> *"One basic tenet of witch psychological grey magic, is that your opponent should never be able to confirm an opinion about you, but should always remain undecided. This gives you a greater power over him, because the undecided is always the weaker."*[44]

Very much a contextual British expression that defines the situation of 'Hobson's ('Hob'-son's) choice, that is the devil's own dilemma; no matter how we shift, it is *'not this, not that,'* neither one thing nor another—

but an in-between state, giving no room to manoeuvre. We are literally 'stuck' there until a result is achieved, and release from its grip is acquired. More than this, the intervention of that severe hand of Fate, whose vice-like grasp prevents any other alternative than the one immediately before us, alerts us to a very gravid situation where matters had accrued that demand our fixed attention. Grasping the cleft stick, we ride the horse. We are literally impotent until inspiration (*Odhr*) offers us the solution to galvanise our requisite shift. It is about surrendering to Her, effectively, to Fate. At that moment, we are propelled inwards and upwards, there to observe the wisdoms received. In yielding to the trap, the sacrifice is complete, we reside, however briefly, 'in-between,' straggling the worlds— the chasm of oblivion and also of all knowledge.

Finally, in its most ancient form, the Stang is merely a Norse and Danish word for a pole. The 'Guiden, like Guidon' means guide, when partnered with the Stang as a pole, the very totemic presence of one's tutelary spirit, by whose counsel we are enriched. And like the process of disintegration, breaking down course matter to render it 'ripe' for planting, like the corn sloughed of all impurities, we are laid bare before the Guiden, processed and fertilised. We are cherished, directed, and summoned to Her banner, as fodder or flax for the making. Before the Pale Guidon, we stand or fall, and as guiden corn, the many are nourished by our blood and bone upon the dark earth.

♦ Merridwen

"Let the Word protect you from the lie- That word is 'Truth.'" [45]

To 'riddle, cast glamour and obfuscate,' are the means of foiling others not privy to the Mysteries of one's own stream of praxis. Truth is ever the hard and complex journey. It begins by stripping the ego through the principles of our mentors. Bowers alludes to this teaching process, somewhat wryly:

"I am very inclined to agree with you about apprentices. People either have the desire to learn or they do haven't. If they want things easy, then it is no use. I find the most difficult job, is teaching them the first basic steps in abstract thought. They all appear to think that **physical** *actions will have* **spiritual** *results ... 'Magic' is all science fiction to the average inquirer, and they bloody well expect miracles with two penn'oth of action and thought."*[46]

Unable to adjust to the profligate indifference to any whiff of meaningful devotion or mystical belief in the generic Craft of his era, Bowers' chose an assertive drive to express his passion for the 'Faith.' Through his beliefs and practises, his work became a curious blend of religion and philosophy, which some say presume to paradox, and yet, as coquette, he woes Philosophy as the 'lover' of Wisdom and Religion. The bonds of belief we are bound to, via the many of our stream before us, by the word, and by sign, all is assigned to Her aegis. But first, we must discover Her key, the hidden code within The Mysteries, the secret kennings of all Craft.

Q: *'My first is an exercise in lateral thinking,*
my second is the seduction of intuitive faculties,
my third extreme sports for intellectual boffins,
my fourth and closing quarter is the yearning for inspired truths,'
what am I ?"
(A: Riddle)

Bowers did of course, make excellent use of the kenning and cunning inherent to all facets of riddling; it was a much favoured arte (known as scoping) by our Anglo-Saxon and Norse ancestors. Inferential concepts draw deeply from poetic references—although Bowers did not use them in the old sense of a direct 'challenge.' Instead, he presented Joe Wilson

I am a stag of seven tines,
I am a hawk upon a cliff,
I am a tear of the sun,
I am fair amongst flowers,
I am a boar,
I am a salmon in a pool,
I am a lake upon a plain,
I am a hill of poetry,
I am a god who forms fire with his head."

This spell-binding chant invokes the Virtue of the seas, the earth and the skies until all become suffused *as 'fire' in the head*. Bowers describes the arte as 'high code.'[51] As an inner mystery of godhead, he appears to name the vehicle of that massive re-construction of the 'self' as *'Merridwen,'* whereby he posits to Wilson, his conclusive view, *"I am a wizard, for I alone transform."* This describes the inner wizard of the psyche, expressed in poesis as the 'sky, creating life out of death.' From his spear (Fire as Lightning rod) thrust into the Cauldron, the (4th) nail of Fate, he draws down from the eternal and unrealised destiny, into Time and Manifestation within the Cauldron that seethes (*Seiðr*).

Therefore it seems unlikely that Merridwen is a typo for Kerridwen, (bearing in mind all Bowers' letters are littered with them); so he has forged a poetic kenning for the inner transformation of the 'self,' an intrinsic gift of reciprocity through Her Virtue *as* Kerridwen; the terrible and relentless Huntress, determined of Her quarry. That Taliesin was triumphant in his own transitional transformation for Her 'Wild Hunt,' was to hold immense significance later when in pressing need, he surrendered himself as prey to Her bow. Speculative suggestions over the years have generated a series of profound solutions to this puzzle with regard to Merridwen and all variant spellings of it. Myth has linked it inexorably to several historical personages. Robert Graves posits his own view when he mentions a 'Merddin' several times within the *White Goddess*; as the ithyphallic and robust Robin-Good-Fellow, Jack o' the Woods, twinned with Oðin in the guise Saturn, or Bran, the All-Father of Life and Death .

Gods of Earth and Sky merge through the central force and fiery fury of Odhr, into the singular character of 'Robin, the son-of-Arte' and for some, the infamous 'witch-god.' Over time, Saxon legend softened the edges of Nordic myth to combine in Robin 'Hod,' where Odhr's man became the 'hooded' figure and Wood-Wose through the legendary character of 'Robin Hood.' Armed with sword, bow and horn, he possesses the symbols and armoury of the king as leader of men; the warrior as protector of men and of the ward and guardian of men. The triune Fool's cap is the Devil's crown triumphant!

Finally, Shakespeare (whom Roy Bowers ardently believed, *'knew a thing or two'*) is able to assert *Hran*, the Herlic figure as leader of the Wild Hunt. His composite character has acquired the horns of the stag, denoting he is the hunter and the hunted; the horn, signifying his role as ward of the forest, guardian of the bounds to the leigh; the horse allows its rider to traverse between the worlds, issuing forth as the oracle and keeper of the 'Word.' He carries a bow that shoots the arrow/dart of Truth, as its messenger. From Ullr, the wintry god of death, we see this spectral form a-gathering up the souls, back to the Mound beneath the great spreading Yews—the Underworld region of the dead. Both- as one, the fiery spirit (Loki) of the Old *Horn* King takes refuge in the form and force of the Young *Horn* King, hence the Tanist dies to himself. As the *'Joulupukki,'* the Horn-ed and *Sacrificial* Yule goat/ram/wren/robin, takes refuge in the Yule Log—of Oak, his totem tree, which is then burned, a gift of fire and light for the hearth. The virtues of the winter yew tree and the decaying oak tree, eventually fused into the common Holm oak, a variety of evergreen oak, whose oak like leaves are sharp and shiny like the holly, reflecting the 'light' of virtue housed there. Holm Oaks were the favourite tree used for the carving of sacred objects and were much venerated in northern climes. It is the most probable species underpins the legends of Yggdrasil.

Natural variance throughout the northern legends across Germania, Scandinavia and Iceland over time and locality, suggest a certain commonality that supports a fundamental Mythos mutually inclusive of all other interpretations. It is sympathetic and sensitive enough of all regional tenets, to absorb the presentation of a compound Mythos formed and preserved through adaptation. Burgeoning craft alliances formed together during the medieval flux, their tentative mystery traditions overlapping where expedient.

Thor/Thunnr is the archetypal hero. He valiantly embodies the Northern mythic virtue of preserver and protector of life. Loki represents re-creation, from dissolution—the dynamic catalyst of change and chaos, as revived from the throes of death. The destroyer, Ullr, Hollr/Vuldr discharges the winter cull. As leader of the Wild Hunt, and gatherer of souls, he is spouse to the great mistress of the benign Hunt: Holda. Oðr/Oðin is the inspiring wisdom, wit and fury—the welter of emotion as the ecstasy, the 'seething' within, of mind and memory, the accumulation of all we 'know' we have been, and will be again. The close companionship established between them, where Loki as lightning (fire from heaven), is drawn to the Hearth. Thor/Thunnr as thunder, the force of the wind upon the waves, and the seasonal rains that fructify the crops upon the land, is also controller of the tides that bring the shoals of fish etc. How earnestly our ancestors realised a holistic, inter-connected symbiosis, as a combined necessity for the welfare of humankind. In this, Loki truly becomes *Merridwen*, 'the pale wizard, who alone—'transforms'—re-creating life from death.

Myth declares that in Gladsheimr, upon the high seats (rokstólar) sat they in judgment. As rulers and governors, the *regin* (*rogn*) took counsel together, offering their bond or hopt, that united all virtue, all forces of nature employed throughout the yearly cycle in Time and for Eternity. These gods, were the shining warriors who, loving men, protected, guided and advised them. Yet their intent became garbled and confused over that same course of time, half-remembered and half-forgotten. This has been a blessing and a bane.

> *"We find ælf, os, god, and, if understood in Old English to denote gods, regen. This distribution is identical, cognate for cognate, to that of words for supernatural beings in kennings for men in skaldic verse and related evidence: ás, álfr, goð and regin. Likewise, the numerous other Old English words for monsters such as þyrs, eoten, puca, dweorg or mære are absent from the Anglo-Saxon name-stock, as are their cognates from the kennings."* [52]

Mjölnir, Thor's totemic hand-staff is described as '*hamarr,*' known in error as hammer (Sanskrit form has it as a stone and sharp, but is in fact, a composite word that better suggests a whetstone and mace/baton/hand-staff/sceptre, rather than a hammer). It simply means 'spirit' tool, a weapon of virtue. Moreover, Thunnr/Thor, known also as *Jólnir,* means Yule figure who presides over that season. Jólnir and M-jölnir are clearly linked through the term '*hamarr*'—the spirit of Yule or Krampus, therefore finds association with the: **bucca, pouk/puck**. As noted in the above statement by Alaric Hall, this indicates how the traditions of the Saxons, though having a basis within those of the Norse, remained distinct enough in language to preserve a purer sense of the divine elements, without recourse to demonising those sacred animistic elements that suffused their worlds.

4
Heritage of the Sacred Ring

♦ The Plough

Legion are the numina, dispensed at the behest of mountebanks where, in contra-distinction, the Word, as the priceless gift to humankind, possesses the boundless power of expansion. Etymology profoundly hints towards our ancestors' observation of Nerthus, whose cart, the Haywain (of plenty), guarded by seven bears secures the biggest and brightest 'Bear' Ward—Arcturus-A, who as Boötes, holds the celestial virtue of Beowulf. One primary tenet of their world-view again empathises the pathway to all error and evil is via a crooked path, whereas the road to Valhalla was straight and true, albeit beset with trials, sacrifice and duty. Bowers refers to 'five or seven stars' as Goddesses. He goes on to equate them with the seven Queens, four within the Castles, relative to the Kings, the Wind Gods, and three without. This is noteworthy and supports another comment Bowers makes on how to approach 'THE' altar:

> *"Before the altar is greeted though, one prepares the ring by imagining a bright star very far away, and above your head. From this star should fall waves of light, and one should imagine that it is getting nearer—or rather you are getting nearer to it. The light should enter your body through the right shoulder, and*

work in a spiral downwards, and emit through the left foot upon stopping to greet the altar. As such the ring, which has been censed and purged by whatever method you use, is charged, and this in its turn becomes a well of wisdom—of the water of life." [57]

The star overhead filters down through the worlds into the Well of Wyrd; here, all formulates within the ring of stones as the necklace and girdle of Brisingamen. Her coronet symbolises Her Virtue, herein manifest within the Compass proper. The Source feeds the Well and we drink from it; from the Cup, we devour all. Any good crop, no matter where harvested, the toil or hazard endured requires the knowledge of the 'farmer' to nurture and evolve the basic yarns, and the skills of agricultural workers to bring all to fruition. Above all, homage is paid to the ploughmen. Nowhere is this better exemplified, than in the stars above.

"There are no hard and fast rules, it must be played by ear. The sense of power is usually denoted by a sensation of extreme panic, then comes the 'gathering' in, you feel that you are being surrounded by a host of 'watchers.' You may possibly see them out of the corner of your eye, these must be ignored and the panic overcome. Then there comes a cold blast of wind, and the power which is being asked for begins the manifestation..."

Classical myth recalls how Boreas, the harsh North Wind, the God of Winter, accompanies Arcturus, the binary gem of the newly risen *Boötes the Ploughman* (though whose cycle is reflected the myth of Cain). Zephyrus, the gentle West Wind, ushers in the welcome warmth and soothing showers of Spring, timed for the rising of the Hyades lodged in the head of the Bull, Taurus. Brightest star of his Constellation is Aldebaran, a follower of the Pleiades, half-sisters to the Hyades. In the ancient myths of the Middle East, we discover links in Babylon between The Bull of Heaven (Taurus) and Inanna, a key element in Her descent to the Underworld. The South wind, Notos, heralds the severe storms and tidal Monsoons of Summer. Eurus, the darkling East Wind, waning God of Autumn (though Autumn as a season did not exist in ancient Greece, Eurus), thrives in Helios' palace in the East, procuring warmth and rain, yet is considered an unlucky wind. [58]

Then as now, Animism pervades our world entire: all life literally and figuratively. Leading on from a gross oversight, it was woefully misconceived as idolatry, a view devolved through a dearth of experience to become, 'idle worship.' Initially, this found further aggravation in residual superstition regarding nature worship. In understanding, we may discern how: *'If the Gods do anything unseemly then they are not Gods at all.'* And yet: the gods, like ourselves are creations of the Divine, they resonate that which is both true and untrue, known and unknown; in ambivalence, their amorality challenges human morality and mortality until we become sifted as the very air itself, rising above all distraction. Thus annealed, we are able to accede to the incomprehensible Mysteries of the Divine thereto find the solace of 'Self.' Only then, via this small mystery, may we travail to know the Greater Mysteries still. Therefore, if we treat those gods as archetypes, we have lost their mystery; and if we treat them as people, then we will never achieve self-gnosis, nor apotheosis.

♦ Ancestral arte of the Vølur

The ancestral stream is also another vital facet to the well-spring of gnosis, tapped through the divinatory arts, as they occur. Most often, this happens quite spontaneously and without the expected 'tools of arte.' The Mysteries are exactly that resonance which distinguishes all gifts of 'divine' communication from divinatory expressions exoterically. That is to say, devoid of a framework, provided in the Mythos or praxis of the seeker. This personal perception is a presentation of ideas regarding the actuation and purpose of the arte magical occulted to acculturation. Within a framework of spirituality and communion with the 'other,' in all forms of mediation that emanate from the divine realms, through all we unveil. Our individual and vital link to all principles of virtue become ultimately realised in the self as Self.

Divination holds an honoured, sacred purpose among all ancient mystery religions; treasures much overlooked in our modern age. Roy Bowers referred to these artes often, stressing the imperatives of poetic and mythic visioning intrinsic to 'true' divination—how then are these to be understood, less still, find expression. Another great observer of the divine, at play within the natural world around him, John (E.J. Jones) was ever the keen advocate of engagement. For him, there was no finer challenge than to seek her voice within the raging elements, as a means of divining. Her pearls of wisdom, whispered upon the winds, and through the actions of birds, animals, the scudding clouds and rays of streaming light, enchant the dreamer, as they lay, fazing upon the forest floor. Softly, she whispers Her secrets upon those sacred winds as harbingers of fate.

In all Her realms is life made known through the magical eye; media sorcery is now Her vehicle for the Word, presented in bounteous array, across the tide of moon and sun. Kalas sheath the subtle bodies with vigour, cleaving prophecy to the ear within. Visions abound the naked eye, wide shut to the world without. Free falling, our limbs loosen to Her strings, pulled downwards, drawn into Her earthen Mound. Slumber then, tarry awhile.

Another pertinent issue John (E.J.J.) attempted to address,[59] concerned tacit associations. He suggested that people should tend towards introducing correspondences cognate to those they wish to emulate, or, at the least, sympathetic to purpose. Substitutions should be considered and designated according to symbology, either by visual, or qualitative association. Alternatives are most often chosen for their

THE VØLUR

symbolic representation i.e., in that the 'fruit' of wisdom is an apple in northern traditions but a pomegranate, peach, fig etc., in other cultures, Wisdom is the underlying theme.

Qualitative symbology is chosen for visual or suggestive parallels, and may even be subject to the *'doctrine of signatures.'* This knowledge and accord will require more thought and research than is generally encouraged. It will certainly demand transcendence of cultural interpretation. For example, to choose a Stang—in either case knowing the function will assist choice of substitute. If the wood is oak in its native tradition, is this because it represents a thunder deity, or because oak is a wood associated with prophesy? Once this is determined, a substitute within an alternative environment should be apparent by studying the culture native to that. Qualities of all the elements are often discovered in obscure association with certain trees around the world. Even here, it is helpful to refine what it is about a particular element you require. Air for example suggests both flight and invisibility, or qualities of the mind perhaps; all of these should transpose easily to another wood.

We return to the divining artes as practised within our numerous northern traditions, where prophecy was ever the domain of the feminine (in nature, the virtue of, and not necessarily of gender). Spoken of and applied through distinctly 'female' forms, there are no male equivalents of expression in those languages. As diviners, and soothsayers, the Seeress or more correctly, the *Völva*[60] belong to a class of women known as the Vǫlur, whose oracular powers are legend within their own cultural traditions. History has nonetheless assigned them somewhat inappropriately under Christianity as *hægtesse,*[61] a now pejorative category that once better reflected their abilities to access the other realms for purposes of prophecy and divination. An almost parallel function served in Greek and Roman culture, via the aforementioned Pythia, ensconced at the sacred Omphalos at Delphi.

Landscape has always provided vital environment for ritualistic activity; for the northern traditions, sacred groves have proven to be the most popular. Trees are, in a nominative sense, frequently subject to punning, where kenning is coterminous with the operative, that is to say the eponymous craft of the Vølur and the arboreal species share sympathetic commonality. One tree associated with the Vølur, is the hawthorn, and is the finest example of this sharing of a language root: *haga* = haw. Over time, such terms have maintained that sacred alliance betwixt tree and female seer. Somewhat likened to the pagan dryadic cults, this was easily achieved, despite negative and prejudicial inferences, implying witchcraft as motivation.

Natural, heathen terms describing Seidr activity, regard the trees (exampled in the hawthorn) **and** the divine presence (odhr virtue) that inspire and infuse the Vølur, as one-and-the-same: *hæhtis, hægtis;* meaning one possessed, driven by the fury of the 'other.'

We find historical precedent in the term: *haetnesse.* As the divine principle of possession (virtue), it applies most particularly, to the goddess forms of Diana/Minerva, falling later to reference a more abusive sense of hag and night-rider, dream weaver and night-mare, then later succubus, the night terror and demoness of Christian folklore. But within northern traditions, this form simply infers a channelling of Wyrd. Having a liminal existence, the Vølur often lived beyond the bounds of the village and crossing that, characterised them as stragglers of the worlds, the hedge-rider.[62]

Within Bowers' 'Basic Structure of the Craft,' there are subtle references to this arte; he mentions the craft of the seer and the arte of divination as relative to the power of place, of dream weaving and of

THE WILD HUNT

Wyrd. We discover associations between the Wind Gods and the elements of Fire in the East, Earth in the South, Water in the West, and Air in the North. Additionally, these support calendrical celebrations or the 'Minor Sabbats,' all sharing a relevance to specific constellations where the sun enters each Cardinal point corresponding to: Spring with Aries and Fire, Summer with Cancer and Water, Autumn with Libra and Air, and Winter with Capricorn and Earth.

Further associations between the four classical elements and the Wind Gods yield fruitful correlations between two distinct systems of symbolism: one being the properties of the manifest realm; the other, the potencies underlying the process of manifestation. How these transpose and interchange and how they synthesise all occulted processes then form the foundational of the Mysteries. Looking at the 'Cross of Elements' we note a further consequence between the square formed when the Jungian vitalities (mentioned in the *'Alchemy of the Compass'*)[63] attributed to the zodiac, intersect the cardinal markers as follows: Spring, Summer, Autumn then winter for completion. This deosil/sunwise motion takes fire to water, to air ending with earth. This forms the 'square' portrayed in the three rites. This marks the themes of the solar rites and how each rite transmutes to the others cumulative succession. Yule literally earths this cycle. The other rings, generate alternative cycles.

> *"...the witch's compass is a highly efficient and scientific machine, and requires science to use it properly...this is the key of kings"* Merkavah—*Sleipnir of the craft...*[64]

In contrast to this, despite apparent similarities, the cardinals denote the winds, whistled up to faze the following pattern, which may be reversed depending upon purpose: East to West and then North to South, crossing at the Centre, the vortex, or Compass Star, formed by the Point (of crossing). Though both appear to follow the same 'elemental' pattern of fire, water, air and earth, they are vastly distinct. The Square follows the emotive qualities of the stellar and solar elements combined as each is drawn forth, each from its natural predecessor (as water/Cancer from fire/Aries, at Midsummer). The Point follows the physical potencies of the elemental winds as they 'rush' in, binding themselves as the central vortex upon the 'point,' the hearth, the *ayin*, the eye of Ra, thereto combine earthly and celestial fire.

The first then, follows the (apparent) movement of sun, stars and moon. The second denotes the cross winds that howl unto the point, the central hearth and Axis Mundi. One is expansive, fanning outwards, the other contracts inwards. One is thus centripetal, the other centrifugal. These correspondences clearly express the shifting nature of the elements, dependent upon how you perceive the element and through what it manifests.

In this, it can be shown how North = Air; but it is also = Earth. Light however, in all forms, most especially of (spiritual) fire (the fifth element), has, in all eras, a singular and quite unique application.

♦ The Woodwose Arte

Roy Bowers declared how he considered no other fate could be worse than the exile of this blessed heritage, a beneficent lineage that is a lifeline in an otherwise alien world. Holding that premise in mind within the theme of Candlemas, he presents a tease in the text of his outline for the ordering of the Candlemas Rite in which Fate holds the space. Her actions as the 'Old Woman,' describe Her doom laden role:—*4. "Elevate platter to Moon. Place contents into pot. Enter Old Man."*

No further mention is offered in the text; but we know that in accordance with the themes germane to this Rite, 'Three Sacred Herbs' are tied in bundles upon the platter. These mysterious contents are chosen quite specifically for their correspondences, their associations to the theme and to the spiritual dimension invoked, echoing quite closely the intent of the 'Ave Maria,' underpinning all acts of contrition and benediction. To honour those associations, we hold as precious, three herbs to dedicate this function. Again, choices are governed by events subject to Fate, including availability, season, climate, personal knowledge, personal choice, and last but not least, in an understanding of the purpose of this Rite. In all things, She calls; and we listen. Therefore, all choices will be deemed valid; each will measure the course and whisper the subtle nuances She wishes us to note, as John once said:

> *"you can adorn the Candlemas wreath with Daffodils, providing you are able to justify it within the Mythos."*[65]

Other specific herbs are chosen for the Poisoned Chalice, for the Sumbel Cup too. Each fulfils a very different criterion of intent and unique purpose. It is the Cauldron that determines again, distinct intent. We should always consider deeply the significance of acts; never are they undertaken in isolation, and always relative to the moment. At Candlemas, the moment consists of concurrent themes of confession, atonement and expiation. Reflected through the means of achievement, we actuate those ideals. Then, in mindful reciprocity, we ally ourselves to herbaceous spirits, nature's glorious paean of souls.

We reverently draw from the earth, the fresh leaves of Hyssop and Rosemary, Rowan and Birch. Rue, the herb-of-grace, adds its own virtue to the bundle; its association with remorse, contrition, and the ability to open the receiver of its benison to sacramental grace, makes its inclusion, almost imperative. This herb of self-sacrifice may suffice within the cup, to loosen the fetters of 'imposed self.' One that may aid the shift of self to Her embrace. Others have favoured Mugwort, Nettle, and Vervain.

71

Within the three herbs chosen, there must be the premise of transition from one stage to another, achieved through intercession, acquired by symbiotic surrender, and obligingly central betwixt the two stages as the 'bridge,' effectively provided the third! The deific correlations with these herbs should appropriate clearly defined links, exhibiting those stages of being, or of states of mind, or of metaphorical and emotional aspects of 'life.'

Compared to Nettle, Vervain holds a similar purgative quality and finds similar association with iron and with Mars, often termed iron-wort, or iron-herb in other languages. 'Verbena,' also named Vervain, used (allegedly), by Romans who favoured it amongst their 'sacrificial herbs,' is sacred to both Venus and Mars. Vervain is another sacred herb to carry the title: 'herb-of-grace or holy-herb.' In his article, John (E. J. J.) notes how the 'Child,' whose name is Compassion, born of Love, is duly honoured, within the Candlemas rites. To reiterate, we need to coalesce all elements through Compassion and Love with relevance to 'Sin-Eating' as an act of sacrificial Grace.

All that may be discovered through investigation is sure to find immeasurable reward for efforts undertaken towards that enterprise. The '*Lacnunga*' is a wonderful resource for Anglo-Saxon Leechcraft. The Lay of the Nine Herbs within it, was always a favourite of John's. [66] It became a recurrent discussion point between us.

> "*Nettle for the 'Old Man' grants a 'baptism of fire' as confession is heard, the fiery, purgative effect of this plant exemplifies the tearing away of sin, internally and externally this plant will set the 'confessor' alight and scorch away the dross. It is interesting to note, the herbs Nettle, Mugwort and Rue are said to drive away 'worms' and 'fought against the serpent.' Alchemically, we may view this through the three elements of 'salt, mercury'/quicksilver 'and 'sulphur.' Nettle would be the initial transition from raw consciousness, material, salt,*

hylic, the sacrificial, uneasy sting of ego-loss. (Nettle in the 'Nine Herbs Charm)."[67]

Crossing the Lethe/Styx, the Ferryman hovers between life and death, in liminal time and between the adverse realities of form and force. Mugwort aids the sub-conscious to relax into deeper fluidity, a mercurial pool, forming a psychic bridge for Kharon to shift between the 'quick and the dead.' Rue, as Grace personified, is the gift of Love in the guise of Compassion. One of the many attributes of nettle relevant to this selection reflects an element of sympathetic magic. It physically represents the alchemical transformation of the spirit, from a 'dross-like' plant of small stinging barbs growing on the wayside to a plant whose fibres can be spun (not unlike flax) to stunning golden hued strands for weaving.

He (Roy Bowers) saw the Magister's responsibility as that which forced each individual to address them (sins, errors, faults, etc), face them, express them and then deal with them. When this is achieved and it can be, it comes from a point of Truth. This pure thought and action, expressed through spiritus (breath) generates the highest Love—that is Compassion, just as Roy Bowers states in his Candlemas Rite. Each person has in this single act manifested Grace, felt, heard, tasted, seen but essentially 'known' at the core of their own being, that part of essential soul attached to 'World Soul' Truly this is a humbling and profound experience for any and all privy to it. If compassion is absent from any individual, they have not transmuted their 'sin' into Grace. So, in this, gnostic sense, together, all students, before and with each other (which includes their teachers) have 'realised' their own expiation, atonement through their ability to sublimate ego through its expression as 'Confession, which for gnostics, means to give breath, to release in spirit.

Vervain's long relationship with Venus as the Evening/Morning Star/

Light Bearer also makes it an especially sacred herb in Traditional Craft and one fitting the Candlemas rite that embraces, along with the Yew on the stang, both death and rebirth. Writing in Sacred Mask, Sacred Dance, John (E.J.J.) stated that the burying of the old ritual year in preparation for the upcoming 'Tides' featured strongly and how it is:

> "*Still recognized in the Candlemas rites when the shade of the old year, symbolized by the old fire, is put out and a new flame lit.*"

Also, interesting as an aside, Culpepper has classified the above herbs in the following governing: Nettle—Mars (fiery smith, agent of transmutation?), Mugwort—Venus (Heralding Light Bearer) and then Rue, Herb of Grace (Sun—Light Revealed). It is intriguing what can be read into such things. The Morning Star/Venus connection is germane to the dynamic between Aphrodite, Ares and Hephaestus. The Magister, cognate in duty to Christos, bears the mantle as mediator between man and his higher 'form.' Grace may be expressed as the pleroma, an expansive force for our spiritual evolution. This is acquired from the divine feminine Creatrix by votive surrender of the male principle to Her Will: Love under Will. Expiration of 'odic' force, or breath, is neutralized through the sacerdotal office of the mediating priest. Prayers and invocations, infuse the primacy of divine force, into the now cleansed spirit.

Each person is and must be responsible for their 'sin' and this profound rite in no way diminishes that. The cathartic act generates pathos and empathy before an invocation of Grace by the Magister suffuses the form (not the force) by it. The original text states only that the Magister (Roy Bowers) becomes the 'bearer' of the 'sin.' This is deliberately obtuse and refers to the principle akin to the 'Confessional,' wherein the 'sinner' is require to vocalise their awareness of what distractions (sin) they have either indulged or surrendered to.

The Magister therefore, in 'hearing them' is able to address them, ritually. Because the Egregore holds all within it, such things become an obligation incumbent upon the Magister as mediator for the hamingja. Anointing by the Magister, as the priestly representative of deity, evokes the *Unio Mystica*. Receipt of the Light of Gnosis, presented as 'Compassion; —the magical Child.' This is realised Grace, or Absolution, a sacred gift of spirit, rendered visible by force taking form within the prepared Host Consequential directives from Roy Bowers' beguiling opening quotation announce:

"Be thou the bearer of my sins," [68]

Clarification regarding the intrinsic importance of all definitions reflecting this view, are absolutely vital before a full and proper understanding may be grasped. We must first explore the nature and significance of sin, and of expiation, in order to follow how they lead to the rites of Purification. For some, this necessitates an uncomfortable descent into themes no longer associated with the modern concepts of religion, or spirituality, which appear in seeming conflict with the neo pagan ethic. Yet they are far from this, as Bowers herein exemplifies. A rounded context prompts awareness of relevant, extant practices within some traditions; without full comprehension of these tenets, Sin-Eating will make little sense. We should be aware of all distractions that may impede the pathway to self-gnosis. The mechanics of this rite seem most appropriate for the task. In solitary terms, some obstacles are easier to rid one's self of than others, especially when using acts of transference, for example—the scapegoat principle. Inanimate objects or simple acts of creation and destruction of an item representing those said obstacles, could also serve.

Other issues may require further insight. In the Candlemas Rite, for example, in his role as sacrificial king, the Magister becomes the aid or tool for release. Many things can block the way, yet it often takes another to yield the impetus to see what form these may take. A noble act yet through sacrifice further wisdom is revealed. Alluded to within operative healings, the work focuses upon the transfer of illness, or bane, to an inanimate object before it is placed at the crossroads. A good example of this in a cultural context, is where the pontiff, as the (literal and metaphysical) bridge is also its guardian, akin to Heimdalhr in the myths of the Norse Peoples. But there the similarity ends. Given his mystical role, Heimdalhr assumes guardianship of the 'Bright Halls' in the divine realms, the heavenly gardens of Edin, of Ida and of Ultima Thule. The High Seat of the Gods and the origin of all myths concerning the Graal, the Platter of Plenty, the Drinking Horn of the gods, the Cauldron of Mead, the Firestone itself.

Exoterically, this figure serves as guardian; esoterically, bridging the inner levels of awareness. In a profane sense, the pontiff degenerates as the unmoveable rock, protector of un-shifting dogma, whereas, Heimdalhr must always accommodate the shift, always sacrifice the moment to eternity. This role of Guardian is clearly, very complex; a paradox in fact, and when adopted by the Pontiff, placed at the Crossroads denoting the foot of the Axis Mundi. Peter's role, as the stone, lies contra to that of 'the Divul,' who, as the rolling stone, reveals how humanity stands between them; Peter, holds the light, whilst the (Divul), emanates light. The immoveable stone and the shifting light, whose shadow falls where it will, blown hither by time and tide. The Craft views this as significant in that one personage holds both torches; their roles combine—they are one, and the same. In a 'tribal' oriented structure, that office unites in the Head-Kinsmen, deceased.[69]

Looking into the myth of 'Peter' (Petra—the rock), we learn that as the foundation for the edifice of Mother Church, he provides the centripetal force; blinkered, it is a ship hurtling onwards, navigating an unchanging and unwavering course. That is to say, it is a path always turning inwards, bearing its force towards a central point—humanity is gathered and pushed to a self-limiting and pre-determined node. Its velocity accelerates into a marked but shallow centre—of darkness. Catholicism in reality, serves to *indulge* individual 'sin,' failing as it does to ensure individual responsibility. No burden transferred; no responsibility taken up. No-one is exempt. The price is paid in advance—a credit extended over humankind in perpetuity. This avails us not.

Within a privileged Mythos, graced with subtle but potent gnostic mysticism, we aspire to a learned history lived as the eternal seeker upon the pilgrim's path. It is enough to satisfy all desires throughout the many levels of our humanity; serving mind, soul and spirit. It is, perhaps, our natural inclination towards centrifugal forces that propel us, drive us, and guide us beyond all boundaries of perception, including that of the status quo. Its velocity pulls us into the pleroma—of effulgent light!

Several important matters need scrutiny here with especial regard to the Clan's ethos, asserting in particular, the issue of strength in the role of Mediatrix. Strength may be appreciated in more subtle ways than as fire; water quenches fire after all. All elements may be drawn upon to offer up their virtue when, and where required. A strong Magister is absolutely crucial to be effective and active, rather than passive. As a true Priest to his 'People,' he will bear their burdens of spirit, yet teach them to work through their own responsibilities of the soul, no matter how painful for all concerned. This distinction assists each person, to work towards true evolution.

Roy Bowers, ever keen to promote evolution of mind, body and spirit within his Craft, was no rock, but a rolling stone. Like Cain, he was a stone whose ripples traversed the web of Wyrd, outwards from the centre, ever further. He was not for stasis, but growth. From a strong hearth, of stout heart, all partake from his rootedness within the Source. As the wind of change, it blows freely. Spirit cannot be anchored thus. It cannot be subsumed in weakness, but only in Truth, Love and Beauty— the Trinity of Grace, or Heart of the Clan. Sin-eating requires more than propitiation, it demands atonement of and by the individual. This is best and ultimately achieved through self-expiation.

Expiation: From the Latin *'expiare'*——Meaning to make amends.

From the Greek *'hilesmos'*—to make acceptable that which will draw one closer to 'god'

To pay a penalty for 'sin' (error), devout actions.

Accomplished through the act of sacrifice itself, profoundly changing the one making it, it stresses the need for each individual to become as or like 'god,' pure in thought, focused and dedicated in service to the divine, viz, without distraction—complete surrender. It is a self-aware act.

4

Tetragrammaton: Sibylline Oracle

Throughout their long exchanges, many analogies passed back and forth between Bowers and Bill Gray, sparking many a magickal challenge as they sought common ground upon which to deliberate their ideas. Bowers motioned the significance of the digits: '1734.' Their exact meaning and purpose find long-debate, still. Among the greater Craft paradigms of the turn of this new millennium, it has become an additional imperative. The figures themselves represent a conceptual equation, a work in progress, not a deity, not a religion, not a practice, but a phrase free of the accepted constraints of tradition (in the sense of a closed system of operation, tied to a particular Mythos, though in the sense of tradition of something that is passed on, it could be). Opinion has and will always discover its own deliberations, based subjectively from the perspective of victory. Finally, from that perfidious platform of all propaganda, projection of that perspective of victory is launched. There is little merit in taking these four digits, irrespective of their symbolism to uphold them as literal representatives of deity, nor should they be viewed as indicative of a religion per se. Rather, they are stages of cumulative awareness of the separate yet conjoined elements within unity.

The Tetragrammaton properly reveals the complexity, and totality of deity through direct experience of each stage/level of its being. In this sense, all methods/processes etc. that elevate any understanding of the Ultimate (from the most mundane to the sublime) via our egress towards it, can be effectively represented by any given or variant form of

IHVH. As with numerous other modalities, a passable understanding of QBL would greatly assist, naturally.

The written word may quickly convey false impressions, lacking as it does all personal inflections or assistant intonation. There is a natural propensity towards subjective bias when conducting research of any kind. Our hard-wired instinct reacts to literal forms, mystical texts and statements encountered. Contra to this, other processes serve the ultimate communication; one media above all others excels in this premise. Bowers seeks to explain the theology of his Faith through the arcane formulae of the *Mask*. To understand how he arrived at his brief explanations to Wilson, Gills and Gray, we first need to consider all that underpins the rudiments of a mystical religion, from all sources that fuelled his genius. This example, like all ciphers, reveals the Word, through gnosis, achieved via inspired insights. It is a method/process of seeing with 'knowing' eyes. Roy Bowers imparted this perspective through all media of word, symbol and image as a symbiotic and osmotic alchemy of the deepest and most emotive profundity.

The meaning and interpretation of words particularly, is always going to be a contentious issue. By bringing to light all possible permutations, our individual understanding is then enhanced and expanded. The danger lies always within the closed mind. A pragmatist would naturally insist upon technical definitions of course, whereas the philosopher might adopt the premise that the meaning of a word is in its use. Our obligation as seekers and explorers, is to consider all possibilities, and through balancing reason with experience, formulate our own understandings. As words change over time, so do all applications relevant to them. What remains critical to seekers and pilgrims, is discernment in their relevance to all we engage; no more or less. Simple elegance is undeniably appropriate to Bowers' inference with regard to his world and to our own. Of course, in terms of industry and alchemy, both word and intent attain empirical status.

Yet, we must err always upon the side of caution. There is of course, a very real danger of tracing a word origin to the point where it is manifest, created of desire, formulating the required answer. As something devoid of real purpose, it may easily become a superfluous weapon in an overburdened arsenal. We have yet to assimilate, or understand fully contextual experience. Once grasped, we may access individual Wyrd, where we may pursue, ever deeper, our accordance within it. At all times, we must be wary of creation and involvement for its own sake, or for vanity, for self-agrandisment. Many creation myths are in fact to a greater or lesser degree 'narcissistic,' even the biblical one. For example, *ex nihilo* (nothing begets something) is good science, the eternal and uncreated is un-limiting and unlimited. The claim: *'desire, the first of all created things,'* articulates how creation is birthed from the dispassionate field of non-being, to the equally narcissistic, gnostic sense of a desire to 'be,' thus falling into manifestation.

To expand and perpetuate one's self as fragments there; or in the love of one's own reflection and desire to be surrounded and embraced by one's self; both, are alchemical actions. In this expansive, all inclusive ambivalence, we range from liberation to veritable suffocation. The Word then, offers to breach the gulf with wisdom or folly. We must choose. It is breath, given *form*. It is wind, or spirit, expressed in a creative manner, rather than a term applied simply as a casual and randomly unconnected principle. Other notable strands of this mode of thought reside in the mysticisms inherent within apocryphal Gnosticism. Bowers makes a few generic references to Sophia throughout his works, though they merely skirt around those deeper concepts held in belief. Insights gleaned from all studious pursuit, may highlight the hidden ethic, weaving its very survival as the idea, and the word into every breath, and every stitch, every mark, and every seed.

The Ophite Cult especially, serves as a valuable resource, plumbed for parallel maxims that may have fuelled the ethos of cultures far removed in time and geography. In that tautalogical regime, their reverence for Sophia set her as the divine hypostatized form of Chockmah. Evolving as Prounicos, She is the Serpent of the Tree. She embodies the Mysteries proper, of salvation and redemption in the Supernal Triad where She is the voice of all.

"Whence dark of night, and ev'n star meet, upon that break, is wisdom's stay;
As Freyja, with shuttle, draws back the veil, to spin the thread of day.
In troth, Her Law, in beauteous bond; tis thus the wise do find their mark,
Dance She will, with ne'r a flinch, to yield your soul, still spinning, of the dark.
With caution, prepare for death; in all due valour thrive, and be forever done;
Fall beyond the pale of Hela's dour realm; then by Her leave; be One.
The path of honour is pure and bloody; no noble man is spared, be bold!
Past conduct meets future promise; a moment bound of eternal Wyrd,
Raise aloft the horn; for weal or woe is the gift of all in duty to behold."

Thrice, Her descent, thrice Her form: as a male, as a female and as the Holy Spirit. In this final form, She relates to *our Lady who will gather us up Home again,'* back to the spinning Castle of Caer Sidi—the Eternal Kingdom. Caer Sidi, turns swiftly upon The Mound, faster than League of all Winds in their haste. Hers is the seat of resplendent fire, the divine throne in this realm of spirit. Many legends claim this Seat Perilous, it is the Devil's chair, Arthur's chair, Druid's chair etc—the Seat of Kings, Kingship and the Holy Omphalos; it is the ancient dancing stone of the Goddess, of Sovereignty, to whom all Suzerains trace their Frith.

♦ Drighton—Hindsight

"I describe myself as a 'Pellar.' The People are formed in clans or families and they describe themselves by the local name of the Deity. I am a member of the People of Goda - of the Clan of Tubal Cain. We were known locally as 'witches,' the 'Good People,' 'Green Gowns' (females only), 'Horsemen' and finally as 'Wisards.'" [70]

Initially derived from the Gaelic form 'Clann,' meaning 'children,' Clan later embraced the term in a less metaphorical sense and began to encompass a broader way of children as a 'family'—effectively a 'People, being the larger unit of a kinship, a description that very much conforms to the social structure of the Scottish Clan/n system. As a collective, based within a specific culture, they shared common customs, most importantly of beliefs, superstitions, folklore and magicks.

"What do witches call themselves? They call themselves by the name of their Gods. I am Od's man, since in me the spirit of Od lives." And "Now, what do I call myself. I don't. Witch is as good a name as any, failing that 'Fool' might be a better word. I am a child of Tubal Cain, the Hairy One." [71]

The Head-Kinsman of a Clan stands as its Chief/leader/father, and in some cases, even as a minor king. A Chief may claim only what is given by this right of heritage, thereafter to 'hold' it in that virtue; no more, and no less than is deeded as title, lands and possessions. His authority and position did not grant him the right to exploit his (sacred) appointment by taking from others amongst his People, anything that was not rightfully his, under the Law.

♦ **Clan Tubal Cain = descendants of Tubal Cain (an heretical line, heterodoxy, a civilising force of evolution)**

This succinct title declares the family as being descendants of a named personage, of mythical or historical origin, in whose stream/aegis the family are now embraced, and by whose current Head-Kinsman rules as Liege Lord in his name/virtue.

♦ **The People of Goda = the priestly line (priesthood of)**

Identity of an inherent cultural premise, a Faith its adherents are hereby avowed to uphold by sacred oath ie: Od's men: The good-men/godsmen; godi/hofgodi; dedicants/servants of the gods of the people: ie "*I follow the gods of my ancestors*"

'*The People of Goda, Clan Tubal Cain*' = 'Hereditary Family bound in Faith to a Lineage of Priest Kings. In other words, a collective people in descent from even older gods when mankind sought evolution under an illuminating avatar—Tubal Cain'

This signifies the Drighton principle of the Virtue of Suzerainty, implementing the right to rule by deed of ancestry, again a contrast to the Sovereign claim to rule by 'divine' right. It is a hoary stream indeed we follow.

> "*I carry within my physical body the totality of all the witches that have been in my family and their virtue for many centuries, if I call upon my ancestors, I call upon forces that are within myself and exterior ... now you know what I mean when I speak of the burden of Time*"[72]

From the 4th century onwards, these Blessed Isles witnessed the influx of migrating tribes from Northern Europe and the Baltic regions, whose settlement here is frequently recorded as violent, at least initially. Specific groups of associated 'Peoples' from those historical tribal systems, having a strong, shared ancestry, established a hierarchy we easily recognise in both Irish and Scottish Clan systems, typifying the structural edifice by which they operate, despite their similarities and significant differences. As a way of life, the Clan system survived on its wits, on its ability to adapt, and to adopt whatever improved upon what they knew. Primarily, its people developed a keen intuition, a canny 'knowing.' Furthermore, through a Faith which enveloped every aspect of their lives, they worked instinctively within and without their natural environs.

"In fact, in the beginning, when working with Cochrane, we were actually practising a rather basic form of the old shamanistic witchcraft without realising it; at the same time, no-one had ever thought of putting it into a more formal footing...the deeper you go into this, the more you realise that the craft is not the be all and end all, so that in the end, you stop being a witch and become a magus, a magician in the old sense of the word."[73]

During the course of so many centuries, the Clans' were entirely dependent upon culture for their survival, dominating all sense of community with its belief in gods. Culture dictates how a people address Fate, particularly how they establish ancestral interaction and observance of those tenets upon which existence is predicated—especially in continuity as a 'People.' That culture is defined today by the bonds and bounds of a systematic hierarchy preserved by those Clan structures extant within the remnants of the guilds and subsequent traditions who warden their treasured ancestry still.

"I keep on getting the feeling that we are preparing the ground for a crop that we will not reap, waiting for a dawn, that will not come, but wait we must ... so far the new word hasn't come through, but it will, that I feel certain of." [74]

These units remain very much misunderstood in our modern world where uniformity is the desired state of being, where individual rights are promoted even as many sacrifice individuality to the altar of homogeneity. In this world, the camaraderie of kinship is as alien as it is incomprehensible. Echoed again, those values underpin the very ethos of Traditional Craft whose origins in the mediaeval *guilds and clans* are discussed elsewhere. Here, we seek to explore the identity and purpose of those peoples, through their work, their lives, in their beliefs; all of which served to cast them under the aegis of a freer elective, an honour bound suzerainty, quite distinct from the restrictive non-elective sovereignty we are currently yoked to.

> "*...this will be a difficult task, since talking about the People (We describe ourselves as such) is a matter that every hereditary group trains out of its members.' The religion is also more, mystical than most—so words are very poor approximations of what we actually discover or feel about our beliefs.*" [75]

History has preserved for us a wealth of material to draw examples from that others may learn of their precedents in a forgotten and neglected heritage. Succession to leadership was never democratic. Neither was it initially dynastic, and least, not in the way we are accustomed to. Custom and tradition were carefully monitored, observing to the letter of the law their strongest tenets in order to avoid nepotism and despotism by encroachment or upheaval. To preserve the virtue of a lineage and of a family heritage, the best protection has always resided in an official and duly appointed heir, elected from amongst the senior, male adults within the family. The Clan, governed by a carefully monitored system known as 'Tanistry,' was ably covered for all eventualities to come. Transference of rulership was generally smooth and without incident.[76]

Preserved by ancient precedents and congress, this law of succession determined from whom, amongst all possible candidates, a worthy heir should be chosen above all over claimants, often with equal and valid hereditary rights. It was almost never the actual son of the current Chief, known also as the Head-Kinsman. Even amongst the (royal) Gaelic patrilineal dynasties of Ireland, Scotland and Man, an elective Tanist would eventually succeed as Chief or King. Many myths and tales recall this arcane system of succession that binds them all within an ancestral chain, wrought within the caprice of fate. Roy Bowers invoked this arcane premise when he announced:

"I cannot die until I have passed my virtue on..."[77]

Again, Bowers continues with the affirmation why this is so…

"I carry within my physical body the totality of all the witches that have been in my family and their virtue for many centuries, if I call upon my ancestors, I call upon forces than are within myself and exterior… now you know what I mean when I speak of the burden of Time."[78]

In spite of this clear declaration of his Faith made by Roy Bowers, concerning the mechanics of his tradition, it has been posited by others that due to the manner of his death, Bowers was unable to pass on his virtue.[79] And yet he did, as E.J. Jones here confirms:

"Roy made me his spiritual heir long before he died."[80]

From within that Clan, Evan John Jones was the Tanist, the leader elected by Roy Bowers to succeed him as Magister of the Clan, heir to the tradition as its Head-Kinsman. Humbly and reluctantly, he valiantly 'held' a position so many have misunderstood. He said of himself, that it was:

'*Hobson's choice, and a poor choice at that!*'[81]

Some have presumed to suggest the leadership of the Clan was intended for Bowers' son, or more incredulous yet, another, unnamed person, anonymous still, leaving the position open and those after him on a tenuous thread. This is an entirely erroneous notion, devised by others not privy to the facts, and unfamiliar with its heritage.

In sharing our knowledge of these here, we are able to show exactly how closely our Clan have complied with and held to these historical precedents and the culture of those traditions. That these details have been hitherto overlooked, misunderstood, ignored and even manipulated, has necessitated their inclusion here. Perhaps through discussion, all seekers of truth and of historical law may finally achieve a level of understanding and appreciation for the traditions and lore of their Craft. Having suffered obfuscation enough, these customs should be revealed in their true light; they have remained buried for far too long. That so much nonsense has saturated the maze, confirms the presence there of far too many lapwings and red herrings, better known as charlatans and snake-oil-salesmen. But, there is nothing new under the sun, and then as now, nothing has changed in fifty years. In their time, five decades ago, the need to expose falsehood by default, demanded bold remonstration. Hence, in protesting the mechanics (and not the faith itself) of another tradition by exposing his own, Bowers broke the customary bounds; as E..J. Jones said of him:

"He was the first of his Tradition to do so."

This entire premise highlights arcane tenets inherent of Old Craft traditions regarding how leadership secures patrilineal authority sponsored through the *hamingja*.[82] A parallel system of operative virtue coalesces matrilineal *geis*. A Potency of Fate alights upon the Lady or Mistress of the Clan, elected by that same force of ancestral Virtue—the *hamingja*, to her. As Seeress she adopts role and title of 'Maid'[83] (through her own line of *fylgja/dis*), bringing the male and female lines together. Again within historical traditions, these were alliances induced and borne by political necessity, having the benefaction of the gods. One complements the other without distinction. Whatsoever is aligned in Fate, is divined as auspicious.

"The Faith is made of three parts—of which I know two. The first part is the masculine mysteries—in which is enshrined the search for the Holy Graal—and is the basis of the Arthurian legends. This is the order of the Sun—the Clan of Tubal Cain…In the distant past, the male clan was lead by a woman who was their priestess and chieftain. This is the origin of the legend of Robin Hood…and the tradition was followed through into the Middle Ages when the Plantagenet Kings were officers of the masculine aspect of the Faith (The name 'Plantagenet' means 'The Devil's Clan'). The effect of the masculine mysteries upon the world can hardly be under emphasized…Law-making….and craftsmen's guilds…The masculine

Herne the Hunter Plunging into the Lake

HERNE THE HUNTER

mysteries were the direct creators of modern civilization as we know it now. It must also be remembered that originally the Mystery was conducted by a woman—and that she was the presiding genius behind many of the fundamental discoveries that created civilization. …The feminine Mysteries are the deeper—connected with the slow tides of creation and destruction, of the cycle of life and death. …The clan of Women is lead by a man, who acts as a priest, and teaches the feminine mysteries …Today, since there are so very few, the old system has broken down and the families teach their children both mysteries, so that the tradition will not be forgotten entirely. In the past the male and female clans were separated except for the nine Rites or 'Knots' of the Year—when they came together and worshipped Godhead. Also, a great deal of traditional rite has been lost—but it will be recovered again one day, since things and thoughts alike do not die, they only change…It was common for the People to meet once a week—like a service or a teaching session, or even to work some particularly difficult piece of magic…and for security's sake the Clans divided and knew nothing of each other. The mysteries were also united so that nothing would be forgotten… [84]

Bowers infers here the loss of the third mystery, the Priesthood. He also speaks historically of the distinction between traditions following either a matriarchal or patriarchal Clan system in eras long past. By no means were all later tribes of peoples invading/migrating to these Isles of one mind. Through personal knowledge of their own distinct arcane praxes, such diversities have subsequently enriched the collective mysteries severalfold. Some of those, believed lost to time and circumstance in the exoteric world, have been preserved by fate within the esoteric realms open to all seekers of the arte. Their retrieval is the Work proper! Of the three original mysteries, the one that more commonly survived is the male mysteries, of law and trade.

These artes were nominally distributed throughout the traditional crafts of guilds, and have barely survived into the 20th century. Craft families preserved what remnants they were able to hold onto to, forming groups loosely based around those archaic Clan systems. Adoption into those hereditary groups is rare and a considered privileged. The Clan of Tubal Cain is one such tradition. Imperative roles assigned to each of the three, secure the merit of distinct yet involved mysteries. Therefore, within our own tradition, specific roles indicate their relationship with those aforementioned archaic principles. The Magister/Master as Head-Kinsman and the Tanist are one and the same through patrimony, and their Lady and Maid holds the virtue for the Clan, hence duty to him under the Law, and absolute allegiance to her, exactly as Bowers stated. She is not chosen by man, but spirit, but man chooses his own successor. The Lady, in her role as Seer, becomes Cup-bearer, and if prompted to do so by Virtue, will accept and acknowledge him. In rare cases, if she feels the heir apparent is not approved by the *disir*, then she can reject the Tanist and suggest another. By the 'Godstone,' she wields the 'Cup and Stang,' by the hearth-stone, she serves them. Hers is the gift of life and death, wisdom and insanity— the true purpose of the 'Poison Chalice'

> "*The Hunter, Old Tubal Cain, and the Roebuck, are one and the same divine presence in the shape of Fate or Wyrd.*"[85]

Whence that Virtue departs her, either by default or death, it is the duty of the Head-Kinsman to seek where that Virtue thence resides, and so it begins again. Exactly as Bowers and Jones lived it, a perfect system with historical precedents. Bowers' Lady vouchsafed Evan John Jones, who 'found,' recognised and celebrated the Covenanted Source of Virtue in the Clan's current Lady and Maid, hailing her as such. Jones selected and appointed Robin-the-dart as his Tanist, vouchsafed in turn by The Clan Matriarch and Maid. Tubal's Mill turns, and another heeds the call to become Tanist to the current Magister; vouchsafed again by the Maid, as tradition demands. That person is Ulric 'Gestumblindi' Goding.

One need not peer too deeply into these traditions to discover them, replete throughout the rich heritage of our folkloric histories and mythical historicity's. Some of these developed from the mythical ages through into the medieval periods and into the eras of strong feminine cults namely 'Marionism and Courtly Love.'

"It is intent and the love of God in creating the magical substance that transmutes it not any particular power in its own right. The best example of this is woman...All females, irrespective of species is a lesser moon reflecting the Greater... Man is individualized and solitary - lead only by reason or passion. Woman by her physical structure is part of the cycle of evolution, and therefore part of the group soul...The woman, as a possessor of this common instinct, shares experience with the group soul—and what she and thousands of others do shapes that soul for time to come... one observes the way a woman instinctively works reflecting the tides of her body, and of the group soul...protection shapes the group entity...Woman is a magical creature, not because of the tides of her body as Graves suggests, but because she has this power to shape the group entity to her desire and following the tides of her soul she creates magic of no small order in making a home for her offspring. It is the Earth Mother working in her deep instinctive acts and she both creates and influences the group soul..."[86]

The Gaels exported their patrilineal system of Tanistry and other customs to those parts of Scotland they controlled after 400CE. The Picts (the other indigenous people of Scotland), did not share the succession principles held by their neighbours of Ireland and of Scottish Gaels. But some exceptions did exist in Ireland. The Picts especially preserved matrilineal Tanistry; in some cases, particularly within those

Irish and Pictish systems, freedom to accept either patrilineal or matrilineal descent, (or even both) was given. A maternal grandson was apparently the preferred heir to grandfather; and/or maternal nephew to uncle. Given the increasing relevance of the connections between the regions of Staffordshire and Buckinghamshire, and of the upper and lower Thames Valley, the Mercian kings' strong adherence to matrilineal descent, is given new impetus. Much favoured by the Picts also, it is significant too that the last four kings, including Offa, married the daughter of the previous Queen.

Within the Saxon Heptarchy, noted also amongst the Germans and the Scandinavians, a similar system of Tanistry thrived, raising the possibility that Scottish and Anglicised regions of Briton must have inherited a bone-fide legacy of Tanistry. Any male relative, even a bastard, may rightfully succeed, in preference to the current Chief's own son. To further tighten the bonds of filial loyalty, fostering first-born children from family units within a Clanship was actively employed, underscoring both extended and unanimous support from cross-linked communities. This procedure ensured a balanced level of inverse equality, a facet of tribalism that those within found immensely gratifying. Community was everything; everyone was connected to each other by adoption or marriagem and everyone was supported and assisted via these honour-bound codes.

> *"The curse of Ol Tubal lies in the management of the Clan itself. You are stuck with it until you feel the need to download it on someone else and when you do, you'll get a tremendous feeling of lightness and relief. In the end you find if you let it, it will rule your entire life and that quite simply is, the 'curse.'"* [87]

Saxo Grammaticus, amongst others, records a typical Norwegian custom concerning the election of a Chief and of his Tanist that very much conform to similar practises in medieval Scotland, Ireland and

Mercia. These sacred ceremonies took place outside the villages near ancient monuments, on hillocks, near erect stones and burial Cairns. Again, we may stress the absence of such rites within woodlands, where rites of a different nature were held. On being elected, the Chief received a sword and a white rod; *"and a genealogical oration was made; while the heir was obliged to give a public proof of his valour before his election."* [88]

Remember, Bowers said:

"I carry within my physical body the totality of all the witches that have been in my family and their virtue for many centuries." [89]

For any leader to place so much trust in his successor, he must first prove his worth. Trials and quests were set to inspire confidence in his choice to their people. Trust in leadership is primary. The Tanist,[90] having completed his task and effected his display of loyalty, would climb up to the 'Tanist Stone,'[91] also named the God-stone, situated upon the boundary, and there declare his trust, a troth avowed before the old gods. Those chosen would typically be drawn from a pool of men, whose own great-grandfathers, grandfathers or uncles had at some point been the elective 'Tanist.' It was common for a son or nephew of a former king or chief to become the next Tanist. As successor he must be of sound mind, a natural warrior, a learned man—a loyal man; one who reflects the virtue to hold the line of kinship: *"the dignity of chieftainship should descend to the eldest and most worthy of the same male-line blood of the clan."*[92] Thereafter, he would effectively be his Chief's right-hand man and even his surrogate when called upon, a heavy office that required a very dedicated and gifted person to fully support his Head-Kinsman. An official declaration of his heir as far in advance of his own death as possible ensures smooth transference of duty—one to the other, vouchsafing the unity of the Clan. Upon these vital imperatives, Bowers refers to the deliberate generational gap between the Chief and Tanist:

"My father, who was agin witchcraft, took one look at me and said, 'Gawd, the old bastard's come back'…and promptly made my mother swear never to tell me the terrible truth of my heritage. However, I had my first mystical experience at the age of five, and since then have progressed in my career. I am a professional, not because I am interested in it, but because it is interested in me. However, after I learned the truth from my mother after my father's death, and then went to see my Aunt Lucy, who is a terrible old woman. She taught me the five artes and the Virtue" [93]

Note also, the imperative of consultation with Bowers' Aunt Lucy[94] to approve his worth. This aligns in absolute accord with everything he'd written regarding the role of 'woman, as the lesser moon' within the Craft, meaning of course, how she reflects the virtue of the Goddess Herself. Through all Her guises, Her many faces and even Her faceless.

♦ Role of Kinsmen

"The path we have chosen was thrust upon us…My Great Grandad was the last Grand Master of the Staffordshire Witches. It has evidently been in the family since at least the seventeenth century, since there are no definate records from that period."[95]

Counting back through those centuries to when the rural crafts of England began forming societies of millers, horseman and masons etc., as remnants of the mediaeval guilds, we are able to explore generational continuity. From within the many generations born between the late 1600s to the mid-1800s, we are able to extrapolate five alternate generations between them, ending in the time frame that fits the claim made by Bowers' for his great grandfather. Though the actuality of this is impossible to prove, the system is observed as true. A context Bowers was well aware of, and speaking of to others with the same understanding.

One very curious custom evidenced within early Gaelic society, informs us of the precedents discussed by Bowers throughout his letters. At least four degrees of kinship generally measured an apical line of ancestry. Welfare, debt and all forms of compensation were the duty of all within those kindred groupings of people.[96] This would change again, and so on over centuries, covering a vast network of affiliated and related families, as People of that Clan, whose name they all bear, even if the patrilineal and matrilineal lines have crossed so far, the actual surnames no longer do.

> "The early Gaelic kin system was a fluid, ever-changing pattern that represented the recent history of the leading families of Scotland. No derbhfine was expected to endure longer than the four generations from the birth of its founder to his great-grandsons. Later generations would be defined by newer kindreds founded on more recent ancestors. As such, the early kin system reflected the ever-changing and evolving pattern of interrelationships that existed between the people and families of early medieval Scotland."[97]

Exclusivity of a dynastic kingship satisfied the Tanist principle maintained by specific genealogies thus preserving a peaceful balance between leading male relatives within eponymous family units.

> "The usual rules for qualification as a roydammna was that a candidate had to be a member of the 'Derbfhine,' a kindred all descended in the male line from a common ancestor (usually a great-grandfather or great-great grandfather). This is recalled in the coats of arms of representatives of the many clans and septs descended from the Uí Néill royal dynasty, many of which feature the Red Hand.[98] The joints in the fingers, the fingernails, and the hand, represented the four/five generations that qualified for inclusion within the Derbfhine."

This signified several layers of information the 'language of the hands' could convey.

> "The language of the hands is complex and I will deal with it much later." [99]

When hands are raised to greet another Clan member, discreet signs are noted, appointed to specific digits and fingers to indicate at a glance the proximity of association, how many generations, and to whom they are aligned.

"Five the [fingers/hand] symbol at your door," a verse from the folk song Bowers describes as demonstrating his 'religious beliefs'—'Green Grow the Rushes O."[100]

Clan systems operated via complex fifth generational rotation, that encompassed a wider kin grouping altogether. This allowed inclusion of even remote relatives, providing they could show a common ancestor, all of whom would offer fealty to their head-kinsman. If loyal, such distant alliances could endure for hundreds of years. Other skills, based in divination and symbology, demanded a competent knowledge and familiarity of the 'language of the hands.' Bowers remarked of these:

"...the vowels are the sacred tree sequence of the North...the Jews had no actual vowels in their language...to write the Sacred Name...The witch holds up five fingers..." [101]

Bowers emphasised to Bill Gray how within his Craft, these rudimentary skills associated with the language of the hands, allowed them to...*"divine with rod, fingers and birds...* "[102]

Clan families, had since their early establishment and adaptations through Saxon and Norse settlements, quickly grown and absorbed others within them. The initial 'four' noted above, relevant to ancient lines of kingship within early myth became established as five in practise.[103] Common Clan/n systems preserved this immensely successful extended pattern of five generations without interruption or waiver for many hundreds of years. Within those, tight, close-knit families and extended communities, ever protective of their gods and their ancestry, the Tanist, must be related, and typically of the second generation.

> *"However, the witch teaching offical line, is that witch blood must be possessed to gain the ear of the gods, and that witch blood re-occurs every second or third generation, and in the same pattern physically. In other words, only witches can bear witches, and to be without the heritage is the most terrible experience of all for a witch. It is literally slow torture. I personally would rather do anything than face thirteen years in the wilderness again; but only another witch would understand me."* [104]

Reiterated below is possibly the finest explanation of what Traditional Craft is and how is operates, and one that conforms seamlessly to historical models of guild and Clan modalities. Bowers explores those duties, the charge to the ancestors, the work itself, mentorship and tradition. Above all, Bowers notion of the mechanics of Clanship, of fealty within the hierarchy as it flows from the Egregore through the principals of titular heads, and then the gyfu of 'return,' back towards the Egregore—a perfect symbiosis. Underpinning his exemplary facet of magickal enterprise, is the grist for the Mill, that is, the true context for the winding of its cogs. Clans became organised into trades and guilds, each possessed of apprentices, customs, rites and lore; each possessed of strict 'family' codes of adoption and rejection. Blood and Bone—the source of virtue within every Egregore!

> *"I in turn recognise the authority of others who are higher than myself, and that authority, once stated, is absolute, do what we may…My job, is to train and organise, fulfil the letter of the law, and to function, to discipline and to curse, as well as to elevate and expound…We have to train any new members to a certain level, develop any hidden power they may have, and finally to teach them how to manipulate virtue. We may be the last of the old school, but we still*

uphold the old attitudes and expect the same. Above we two rises another authority whose writ is older than ours, to that authority, we give absolute allegiance, and whose function it is to train us and work with us…I was in the fortunate position of having been blooded, therefore I have some hold on their ears."

From what dynamic did the current phalange of offices within the Craft inherit roles, honed through centuries of social evolution; remembering of course that these habits set the precedent for all custom and folklore that followed? Custom has maintained the core tenets of the arcane traditions for these lands, and even though only half-remembered, they remain a priceless source for those who now seek their inherent mysteries. It is fascinating how the parallels between these early martial hierarchies form a near perfect graft upon the Clan regime of office, and then how these are further caricatured within the roles adopted by the Mummers. 'Folk' lore and law indeed!

♦ Clan Structure—The Mysteries

"The secrecy of these Masters has nothing to do with protecting the Mysteries, since all that can be said about the Mysteries has already been written into folklore, myth and legend. What is not forthcoming is the explanation."

Medieval Barons worked hard to maintain the high bar set by the Great Chiefs of Old, continuing to observe the Law of Hospitality, of protection, of duty and care to all those under his aegis. Their livelihood and well-being, ever at his behest, ensured a full purse, a roof over their heads, and a warm hearth around which to gather and feed their own families in return for their loyalty. In like manner of these blessings, the customs of our northern ancestors, the right of feasting on the Chief's benefaction have proved a consistent symbol of high privilege, and more assuredly, of a rare liberty.

During the Viking Age, Clan leadership shifted dramatically into an increasingly militarised faction, where 'rank' formally defined your role within an ever expanding society, at risk from engulfment from society as an homogeneity. It is somewhat ironic how constriction generated freedom, a release that revived mercantile wealth, cultural tolerance, economic and artistic growth. These are the threads from which the extant tapestry of Craft hangs by, threadbare, faded, but attached to roots that stand firm. Threads may be traced back, picked up and darned, re-working the bonds of the new upon and through the bounds of the old, as is meet to do so. And what do our skeins reveal? In order of hierarchy, after the Head-Kinsman, Chieftains, from whom the Tanist/*Toiseach* found selection, each headed their own individual houses or smaller family units within the Clan proper; these collectively formed a Clan. A Clan Captain could be selected from any family; this was an office chosen by the Chief according to his worth.

"The man I work with is called John Armstrong, and he is an actual descendant of the Armstrongs of Cumberland and Durham. Armstrong was not only a bandit, but also a chieftain of no small merit." [105]

Composed of earls, chieftains all in their own right, therefore each holding an hereditary office, this historical body politic, pretty much set the court regime, consistent with their own eras. These were the men in fact who once set an historical precedent when they defended those rights against a tyrant king, forcing him to sign the now infamous 'Magna carta,' whence he attempted to dissolve those rights. That document has been woefully misrepresented ever since; protection of the rights of all men is one task it was certainly never drafted for—only free men of means. And those 'free-men' were hereditary earls. In times of war and conflict, these would be the men the head-kinsman called upon. Martial Law superseded all others under those tenets.

To declare separate yet bonded identities, each house or lesser family within or aligned to the Clan expressed their loyalty that inspired later heraldry. Clothing and armoury presented an instant marker to be noted and accounted, especially upon the battle field. Banners, tartans, sashes, badges, charms were worn and carried, drums and pipes trilled out alma maters and voices rang out guttural cries to make the very dead rise from their graves to follow them into the fray.

"The principle of obedience is said to have consisted in voluntary attachment, not in force; while, in subservience to this devotion, succeeded an attachment to the Chieftain."[106]

We may distinguish between the nature and social standing held by Chiefs otherwise known as the 'Head-Kinsman' and their Chieftains. The former, as head of an extensive Clan comprising of several sub-divisions, bore authority over the latter, who were duty bound as members of their collective tribe, held in allegiance to him. Therefore, as Head-Kinsman and overall Chief, Laird, Liege Lord, and Drighton, he alone was the *Ruler of Law*. Devotion of duty, one to the other was a matter of sacred trust, held in troth between a Chieftain and his people, held in troth in the establishment of gyfu.

The nine noble men thus epitomised the nine noble virtues as essential foundations for later ennoblement and used most frequently in the construct of court dynamics in myths and legends:

1. Chief—Supreme Leader and Lawgiver

2. The Tanist—Nominated by the Chief

3. Tanistry was a system of succession by a previously elected member of the Clan or family.

4. Commander/Military Leader

5.   Chieftains—(heads of various branches or Septs of the clan, always appointed if the Chief were old or infirm)

6.   Gentlemen—(those who could claim a blood connection with the Chief)

7.   Clansmen—The greatest in numbers

Duty was awarded first to their Lord, then to their ancestors, then to each other, then finally to the people they protected with the families of their Clansmen, and other clans or tribes they may be aligned with. Family history was awarded particular reverence. Caesar carefully noted the role of officers appointed to maintain certain elements of culture and law, and how this was celebrated and honoured. These pertain to the seven + one important roles his bodyguards in various guises composed within his personal retinue, whereupon the Chief made ninth man. We have here the names of those roles in Scottish. Alas, their cognate terms in English are lost to us except as correlate titles awarded within esoteric chapters, lodges, groups and brotherhoods. Their valiant attempt to preserve them allows for valuable research into their precedents and purpose. In turn, this allows us to embrace them with full understanding within the traditions and customs we follow still within our chosen modalities of praxes. They stand as follows:

1.   The Guiden or Standard-bearer;

2.   The *Gilli-more* or Sword—and armour bearer;

3.   The *Cockman* (Gok-man)[107] or Warder, the Sentinal, who watched night and day, he who called out from the shadows *'who goethe there'* into the shadows yonder;

4.   The *Hanchman*, or Valet, who would attend his chief at all times, standing behind him at table to ensure no insult befell his chief,

ready to defend him even at every point and turn of phrase. Three other servants completed the entourage,

5. The *Gilli-comstraine* (leader of the King'/Chief's horse over difficult terrain);

6. *Gilli-casflue* (personage entrusted with carrying the Chief across ditches and rivers in the absence of a suitable bridge) and

7. *Gilli-trusharnish* (personage entrusted with carrying all other personal baggage of the Chief).

Within the 'troup,' or coterie surrounding The liege Lord or Drighton, is one other, the *Bladier* or 'man of talk.' His role offers us an intriguing possibility that he could have been serious as in the way of a Scop, Bard or Skald, or of folly as in the jester, the fool—hence the bladder carried aloft in all Mummer's Parade's to this day. It was a solemn undertaking to recite the heritage and lineage of a Liege Lord, and in battle, the cry to arms included this weight of ancestry. It must be added too, that the *Bladier* would equally mock and taunt all opponents upon the field.[108]

Even then, who is to say these roles would be distinct? The recitation of history in prose and verse was the cornerstone of all culture, focused literally around the hearth itself. The roles we witness then in the Mummery of festival evokes by default the shadow of an earlier pattern? The long cherished Clan system officially disappeared from active political formation, drawing to a close a system of cultural ruler-ship that had successfully evolved over twelve hundred years in some regions before those systems officially succumbed to feudal law, defeated by political conquest.

"The inherent philosophy of the Craft was always fluid, and fluid it must become again before it gasps its last breath under a heap of musty nonsense,

half-baked theology and philosophy. Witches cannot retreat from the world any longer, there is no room for us in this society unless we have something valid to offer it, and participate in its social evolution."[109]

Matrilineal and Patrilineal Clans of Pictish, Gaelic and Norse origin had very much enjoyed their autonomous rights to rulership, dependent upon their individual cultural heritage, but these suffered erosion during the 12th century when English court influences connived to abandon those traditions in favour of others more dynastic, of hereditary sovereignty.

"The fundamental difference between the clan system of society and the feudal system which was destined to supersede it, was that the authority of the clan chief was based on personal and blood relationship, while that of the feudal superior is based upon tenure of land."[110]

Old Gaelic lords swapped traditional titles of *mormaers* and *toiseachs* to become '*barons*' and '*earls.*' Under the Norman feudal system, a considerable power shift occurred that many took exception to. Feudalism decreed that everything and everyone within a kingdom belongs entirely to him. Upon the hierarchical ladder, everyone was a vassal to the man above him, except the king who became the vassal of god, hence, the instigation of 'divine' kings began.

"The coming of the Normans to Scotland also brought a new idea of the family group, and a new pattern of inheritance based on primogeniture in land and title. Inheritance was no longer split amongst the derbhfine, but was passed directly to the eldest son. Gone was the old system of shared rights to the family land. While a Gaelic Tanist would inherit only the share of common land which was allocated to him, the feudal heir inherited the whole estate from his father—his household would include servants who might be relatives, but they had no rights of inheritance and owed their livelihood entirely to their lord. The

derbhfine, the traditional extended family with its shared landholding became a power block, under the rule and ownership of a single man. And whereas the shape of the derbhfine had changed with each passing generation, the new feudal family power block could pass unaltered from father to son." [111]

Scottish society was greatly challenged by this influx, changing the manner operated by the Clans from one that encompassed a broad fold to one that focussed on the *derbhfine*, the smaller unit surrounding the founder of a Clan. The imposed system utterly destroyed the honour bound system of gyfu between a liege Lord and his men, and indeed by extension, his people.

Reviewing history through this enlightening perspective allows for greater clarity when regarding those events surrounding the alleged treacheries of Robert the Bruce,[112] Macbeth, King Stephen, Richard III and others whose actions may now be better understood. By Tanist law, these men were rightful kings, an 'entitled' position denied them by hereditary, monarchical rule. Their plight, presented by historical bias as usurping through covetous acquisition, should be contextualised so that the politics and law of their own time better reflects their actions in a changing world. They were not the first, nor shall they be the last to balk at sweeping change, the flux and tide of upheaval, rebellion, and war. It is noteworthy that as a precedent in the lines of succession, the Tanist system was raised and evoked until it was finally abolished by royal decree, by James VI of Scotland, Ist of England, thus making the arcane law of these Blessed Isles, pertaining to the rights of heritage, illegal.[113]

Once disbanded, their practise was eventually outlawed by English Monarchical Sovereign rule implemented above. Shortly after its implementation here in England, newly imposed English common Law replaced the now outlawed Clan and their Tanist traditions in Ireland.

Abolition finally reached Scotland, after Culloden, decimating arcane tradition at the source.

> *"Some groups seek fulfilment in mystic experience—this is correct if one does not forget the duty of 'involvement'—the prime duty of the wise. It is not enough to see The Lady, it is better to serve Her and Her will by being involved in humanity, and the process of Fate (The single name of all God's is 'Fate'). In fate, and the overcoming of fate is the true Graal, for from this inspiration comes, and death is defeated. There is no fate so terrible that it cannot be overcome—whether by a literal victory gained by action and in time, or the deeper victory of spirit in the lonely battle of the self, Fate is the trial, the Castle Perilous in which we all meet to win or to die—Therefore, the People are concerned with Fate—for humanity is greater than the Gods',* although not *as great as the Goddess. When Man triumphs, fate stops and the Gods are defeated—so you understand the meaning of magic now. Magic and religion are aids to overcome Fate, and Fate is a cradle that rocks the infant spirit."*[114]

Larger Clan structures had exerted their influence through kinship families forming extended communities that often settled collectively, for support, defence and continuity of their subjective cultures. Rivers, historically denoted natural boundary markers, both locally and regionally. Gewisse, according to *Bosworth Saxon Grammar,* as a descriptive rather than a noun, suggests 'surety.' Extrapolated from that steadfast 'certainty,' others have translated the term to infer possession wisdom, of a 'knowing' and to have a (certain) 'strength' of purpose and duty, and also a reliability—especially to 'stand.'[115]

> *"Original typologies for early Anglo-Saxon artefacts were based on Bede's belief that the Adventus Saxonum was a single event, occurring about 450AD. As we now know, Bede was mistaken in this; Germanic settlers had begun to arrive in England more than a century earlier."*[116]

106

Earls of Mercia were heirs of the *Hwicce*. In that heartland, the Staffordshire Hoard was discovered in the first decade of the 21st century. Consisting largely of gold sword ornamentation, traced by its decorative artistry, the hoard dates from the end of the seventh century, during the period of Northumbrian occupation. What is most fascinating is that the gold's origin is India, confirming sure trading networks and more importantly, cultural and language influence resulting from those trading contacts. Curiously, Bowers does actually refer to the Hwicce[117] as traders of salt, and makers of cheese: merchants and purveyors—the beginning of the Guilds operatives. As a Saxon tribe, the *Gewisse* re-located to the Thames Valley in the latter part of the 6th Century. Within the *Anglo Saxon Chronicle* they claim their name through ancestry to 'Giwis.' It has been asserted that this tribe may have links to the *Hwicce*, and even a common origin in their homelands prior to migration.[118] A Brythonic origin is also given that offers an alternative etymology for *gewiss*, derived from the word *gwys* (to call or summon) given definition in the form of *Y Gwysir* meaning: 'The Summoned.' [119] Those who heed 'the call' perhaps? Two eminent dons composed a wonderfully succinct maxim that could certainly be applied to much that is presented as fact right across the board. However, they posited that:

> *"What we know of the early Saxon period is largely speculation which has become hallowed by repetition."*[120]

Written retrospectively, literary sources are mere fragments, remnants of heroic poetry that survived oral demonstration before their eventual written forms were preserved, compiled alongside others within later manuscripts. These are chiefly historically based, the best examples are to be found in the *Epic of Beowulf* and the *Ynglinga Saga*. From these we are better able to re-construct the life and times of Germanic Tribes and early Clanships naturalised within these Isles. Primarily, we are able to evoke the law and code such peoples lived and died for in a world where both depended upon your lineage, the very blood that either ran through your veins or under whose aegis you became adopted. Prowess in battle, camaraderie, fealty and the law bound all brothers-in-arms as warriors who ate and even slept around the great hearth. Known as the *'heorth werod*,'their existence was intrinsically bound in 'gyfu' an honour bound code marked by ring-troth and sword vow.[121]

> *"The Faith is a belief concerned with the inner nature of devotion, and finally with the nature of mysticism and mystical experience. It has, in common with all great religions, an inner experience that is greater than the exterior world. It is a discipline that creates from the world an enriched inward vision. It can and does embrace the totality of human experience from birth to death, then beyond. It creates within the human spirit a light that brightens all darkness, and which can never again be extinguished. It is never fully forgotten and never fully remembered. The True Faith is the life of the follower, without it he is nothing, with it he has contained something of all creation."[122]*

5

Providence

◆   **Hand of Fate in the Round of Life**

"The Maiden is the daughter of light, Upon Her, stands and rests the majestic effulgence of Kings, In the crown of Her head, the King is established."[123]

Five Gifts (of Perception) intuited by Roy Bowers, were gifted by Her during his experiential explorations into the Mysteries of his Craft. Despite a life short in years, he enjoyed full measure of experience within them. He grasped the cycle of life, which he concluded as the five principles of comprehension, saturated with *mystes*.

To corroborate this foray into unchartered realms, Roy Bowers extends to the student, five separate proofs; though he is at pains to define them as non-intellectual exercises, but experiences of force. Stressed as empathic realisations borne of direct and unequivocal visionary contact, he describes their principles as follows:

'Force requires form at this level of being, therefore ritual exists to contain that force. Godhead demands worship, therefore ritual exists to give and formulate that worship. Man needs help, therefore ritual is designed to give that help. It is possible to comprehend Godhead or Force without ritual, since the First Principle of Godhead is present at all levels and in all things at all times—but total perception is not present in humanity all the time.

Therefore ritual basically becomes a matter of increasing perception until something of Godhead is finally revealed, and that which is within and without

PROVIDENCE

is partially understood: comprehended in the physical person of the participant until it becomes one with his total being. The forces comprehended are part of the living person, incorporated into everyday life as part of a spiritual, mental and physical discipline that returns the devotee again and again to the original Source." [124]

♦ Wyrd: The Overcoming of Fate

By way of analogy, the better to understand the draft inculcated into the inspiring meld that affected Bowers so deeply, we are bound to study further his own appreciation of his Muse. She, who haunted him, She, whom he declared as the highest of all things, ruling over all gods. Wyrd, as lone sister, carries many of the attributes of the Pale-Faced Goddess. Older than Time, She is eternal, of sculptured alabaster. Her passionless face finds animation only in her piercing eyes, staring out beneath lustrous curving eyebrows, icy sapphires bright with the Light of Ages. Hard as Moon-shine, glazed as steel, they shutter all wisdom's hoard behind them. No furrow mars Her glorious features. Her raven hair forms an ebony veil, falling to Her feet. Her long proud nose arches over full and sensuous lips, red as blood. Parted slightly to reveal teeth as white and pure as seed pearls, we are reminded how She is the one who lines Her nest with the bones of poets and others, fallen asunder to Her lunar magick. In this guise, the Goddess keeps the Cauldron invested with all the attributes of Wyrd. A central symbol of the Craft in all its traditions, the Cauldron contains past, present, and knowledge of the future. It is also the vessel of wisdom and inspiration. When we drink from the Cauldron, we can gain a measure of that knowledge, providing, of course, that we remind ourselves of the inherent danger in drinking from it. The Cauldron, like the Well, symbolically contains the medium of generation in the form of new ideas.

We look upon the Cauldron as the pool of existence in a truly mystical sense. Holding in suspension life past and life yet to come, we return to it in death to await our eventual rebirth. The image there engraved of the horned capped Jotun, suggests the figure of Loki, who is ever the loyal and erring servant to the 'First Cause.' Dipping souls into the mighty cauldron, they are re-created anew, as warriors and tribal leaders, each sporting their own totemic helmet, likened to Beowulf. When we are reborn from this pool, we each face life anew with all its triumphs and tribulations, all joys and all sorrows. We continue to live, in action and re-action to events and circumstance instilled and remembered from those previous states. Hopefully, with the wisdom of hindsight (consciously or sub-consciously), we may glean deeper intuitions when faced again with further trials and tribulations, knowing how best to act in the 'rightness of things.'

Little wonder that when we portray the Goddess, we show Her seated on a throne with two of Her sacred geese, one at either side, looking up at their mistress with adoring eyes. She sits calmly, dispassionate and infinitely remote, with an air of detached sadness tinged with compassion. For She is the one who knows the ultimate Fate of our world because She is the one who ordained its weaving into the very fabric of creation. Even when that Fate finally has been played out, She will still be there, the Alpha/Omega of all creation. Therefore, in laying all before the reader concerning Fate, we may follow the pattern She weaves throughout our cumulative works.

> "It can and does embrace the totality of human experience from birth to death and beyond. It creates within the human spirit a light that brightens all darkness, and which can never be extinguished."[125]

Fairly stated, the Clan's Mythos engages a substantial mystical predilection, primarily due to its absorption of indirect and rather gentle gnostic influences, yet drawing of others equally important. Over time, its evolving ethos favoured the 'oak and the wren' to the almond and star of the east. Cultural origins borne of northern traditions in their flux, eased their way into its Crafting. Forged together thus, slowly and meaningfully, their organic subtleties added layers that challenge and defy an absolute definition or description; even today.

All labels fall short whence true work upon a devotional path is lived as more than a vocation. Mysteries endure for the earnest seeker and pilgrim of craft, arte and mystery. From those medieval resonances, an amalgam of mysticism and English folk culture sprang forth; fundamental principles birthed a stream of cogent belief. Bowers' maintained it was a Faith which had preserved the last vestiges of the real Mystery Traditions. As hinted previously, an era of tidal flux presented an historical precedent. In that period the fertile ground for growth in all crafts was seeded. Enriched by Medieval tenets of heroism combined with sympathetic facets of Marionism, the blend was uniquely opportune for the absorption of complementary and cognate streams of wisdom based ancestral folk magicks. All resolve is fought and won in the arena of life, where we are ever mindful of Her Providence; thus placing a new spin on *fate and the overcoming of fate.'*

For if we overcome all that life places at our door; then we can say with absolute conviction, that we have released those 'fetters' that bind us to this pre-set realm, from an existence that withholds further access to higher realms only through ignorance of them. As the measure of one's life and one's Fate, we seek most earnestly to 'overcome' such restriction. Through the work, through living the Mythos, through being within its traditions, then, and only then, will all wisdoms be gained through love of Sophia in all Her guises, allowing passage through Her bonds, the gateway of aspiration. In this way, do we 'overcome' all (self-imposed) limitations. 'Bonds' formed by these virtues are in truth threshold barriers. She, being Divine remains unaffected by them, for of course, She is Boundless!

> *"Mysticism knows no boundaries. The genuine witch is a mystic at heart. Much of the teaching of witchcraft is subtle and bound within poetical concept rather than hard logic."*[126]

Middle-Earth, or Midgardhr, veils allusion to Hela. Mystics will surely recognise Her hand in this portal of life, by whose aegis we are indeed 'bound.' Those who choose to follow 'the Faith' expounded by Roy Bowers, will discover the sublime mysteries unfurling in their devotional acts of living, where 'all ritual is prayer.' Absorbed together over time, they are distilled and reified, evolved and above all treasured, lived and hailed. From these firm foundations, it can be discerned how those realms above and below this one of corporeality, have left their mark, where clear influence defines its Covenants and Works abiding within the totality of its parts. Directly and indirectly, our folklore and cultural traditions typify those our northern ancestors traversed, in whose worlds *we* now traverse, invited with gentle steps. There we walk with giants in 'other'-worlds, seen and unseen; for:

> *"All is One and One is All, and ever more shall be so."*[127]

Here, in ambivalence do we walk the plane of 'Hel,' a realm wherein we learn to seek out those of the 'Other,' to know them and to grasp what lies beyond, around and within, ourselves, and within this realm of earth, so perfectly placed betwixt and between, that all might co-exist and be 'known,' inseparably—as One! Most importantly, we learn how to live, to be alive, to love; and best of all, how to celebrate this brief, material existence as their gift to humankind, that we may know them by their deeds, and they, by ours. In this land of heroes, maidens, dragons and monsters, we see the mask of god and of the self; guides along the straight path, onto and over the bridge home. Until that point of stillness occurs, we engage chaos in all forms. All around us, other worlds spin with opposing forces. Pulling on each other, they generate the necessary impetus to stimulate change, the tidal flux of evolution, the bright and dark gods, elves, giants, all mirrored in the gnostic lens as aeons, archons, *nephelae* et al.

> *"It is a religion mystical in approach and puritanical in attitudes. It is the last real Mystery Cult to survive, with a very complex and evolved philosophy that has very strong affinities with many Christian beliefs. The concept of a sacrificial god was not new to the ancient world; it is not new to a witch."*[128]

Myth suggests no less than 49 creations of beast and spirit, ruled over by the trickster, named for Loki, or any other aeonic form. Principally, they share similar cosmogonies where watery light, challenged by luminous fire, fuses, generating corporeality. The realm wherein that creative spiritual spark is similarly challenged by psychic forms and by hylic forms evoke wisdom in all Her forms. Death, androgynous and eternal, haunts our reality, replicating life by palingenesis. According to gnostic perception, these lower, hylic counterparts do not share in celestial immortality, named for their own counter virtues. Promethean fire is shared judiciously with the seven (Planetary) heavenly kings after which it passes through the five elements to manifest as Fire of fire, Fire of ether, Fire of water and Fire of earth. Twelve 'fires' in all, seven Celestial, and five Sub-Lunary.

These numbers are immensely significant, and will be clarified shortly. Of the 7 kings, we discover three named for Cain, for Abel, and for Athoth/Death & Limitation/The Reaper (Saturn). This very much suggests the Old and Young Horn King, inclusive of the Tanist within. All seven encapsulate individual prowess through a totemic beast indicative of inherent Virtue. Despite the vision of Saturn as the reaper, the farmer and keeper of all knowledge pertaining to animal husbandry, he is oft likened to a sheep. For *Cain* (Mercury), a Monkey; and for *Abel* (Moon), a beast known as 'fire-face.' Tentative cognate forms may suggest Cain as the 'Lunar' ape of Thoth, (Hermes), the Tanist counterpart to Abel's natural Lunar symbiance, via *Sin*, the All Father.

Lunar roles in the arcane world were almost exclusively 'male,' a noteworthy factor relative to the placement of sun and moon common to many northern traditions, though not all. Pertinent here, is Bowers' enigmatic comment to Bill Gray, in which he motions adversely to Gray, the use of labels, deferring Clan descriptive epithets on principle. He states, rather baldly, that though our Mythos presents names and forms, they are naught but 'close approximations' for their real virtue. Moreover, behind those epithets, all titles may find other cognate triadic forms, most typically expressed respectively as: The Reaper/*Saturn;* Thoth/*Hermes* and *Hekate* as Barbelo, the Mother of All—(whose gnostic cognate is matched in the Tri-morphic Protennoia).

Her Source is accessed either during vision quests, mystical pilgrimage, or as souls in transit after death; these are often turned back, unless special conditions are awarded by guides or gods, dependent upon tradition or system of belief. Fate is the hardest of all material causes to overcome, the deepest bond and the most tenacious. Wound so deftly into our material form and life, the charge to overcome it runs parallel to living life; it is the darkest and yet, the most blessed gift of the gods. There is no contradiction here and no conflict. Both are gifts; we are ever mindful of the pleasures both realms afford us.

> "*Within the disciplines of the Faith, man may offer devotion to the gods, and receive certain knowledge of their existence by participation in something of the perfected nature of godhead, recalling that both within and without, which is most true.*"[129]

116

Yet to attain those higher realms, some measure of sacrifice and work must be engaged in order to gain the necessary wisdoms to pass in to those fabled glittering halls, thereto sit and feast with the gods; thereafter to succumb to sublime existence, blessed within the godhead for all eternity. Words and signs needed to confirm that 'elective' wisdom, combine intent within the magick of seals and sigils. In their utterance, the sonic resonance invokes the gods of one's father's, father's father, and so on; thus are we known and recognised as kith and kin. Our re-absorption back into either realm is dependent upon the success of our mission in life, subject to an all-consuming activity, analogous to corpse-eating: a demonstratively apparent figment of folklore attributed to an uncommon myth concerning Níðhöggr.[130]

"All the things eaten in it themselves die also. Truth is a life-eater. Therefore no one nourished by truth will die..."[131]

Looking a little more deeply into the personage of Barbelo (all wisdom), we discern yet more elements coterminous to some inherent to our Mythos. Again, not strictly gnostic, the Mythos nonetheless retains trace influences, absorbed from a deeper layer of its cumulative histories. As *Tri-morphic Protennoia*, Barbelo's tripartite nature is revealed; *'She became the womb of everything.'* Theology records this form named and referred to as *'He,'* hinting again at the higher and supreme androgyny of The One, the Source of All that exists in purity (from corruptions not assigned to moralities, for the gods as creative forces are amoral. And so it is, that Barbelo becomes both Father and Mother of *Aeons* (all forms and intermediaries of the material realm, being subject to Time).

"Thou (Barbelo) didst continue being one (fem.); yet becoming numerable in division, thou art three-fold. Thou art truly thrice, thou one (fem.) of the one (masc.)"[132]

Barbelo, now unified, undifferentiated, is Tri-morphic wisdom supreme. Expressed analogously through more familiar classical forms as:

- Fore-thought of the Father (Pronoia);

- (Protennoia as); All-thought and;

- (Epinoia as) Afterthought or Hindsight.

All truly great things hold fast as a 'Trinity,' Hermes Trismegistos and the Holy Trinity are the finest examples of this. We may now return to place in context, the succinct quote where, as the Silence, the divine Sophia; Protennoia pronounces of Herself all the characteristics Bowers assumes in the figure of Hekate:

"I dwell within the Silence (as Time, Fate etc, being the laws of Chaos) that surrounds every one of them."[133]

Hence, as All, Mother/All Thought/Wisdom (Barbelo/Hekate), She carries the full virtues of Forethought as (Oracular Vision/Providence/Fate); First Thought (the eternal now); and Afterthought (Hindsight and Memory). Her eternal forms of expression come through the flight of birds, swans, geese, falcons, owls, doves and ravens. Huginn and Muninn, Her ravens as cognate selves (fore and aft): as Fore-thought/sight and After-thought/sight. She gifts these to Oðin as Wards of Time and Fate to accompany Him upon his eternal wanderings. Under that root which turns then toward the Rime-Giants, is Mím/ir's Well, where hoary wisdom hides. In this murky place of ancient lore, Mím/ir, the titanic giant preserves the Well, drinking from it by the Gjallar-Horn. Thither came All-father, craving one drink of the Well; but not until his sight is given in pledge, which eye, and to what extent His sight is impaired, is never clarified; only that he is (metaphorically) 'blinded' and from this, hereafter is known as 'One-eye.' A strange token, yet wisdom is gained only through the balanced combination of Hindsight and Foresight.

His sight, gifted to Mim/ir, appears to suggest an ability to 'see,' an especial kenning, referred to in mystical terms, as the 'mead of inspiration.' It is the kenning virtue claimed by Bowers to: *inspire our inherited wisdom.* It the active (fore)thought, metaphorically perceived as the 'Sun,' which takes form as the 'Fallen;' His sacrifice to mankind, and mutually, theirs to His. One prized facet of this manifests as the legendary crystal known as the Sunstone. The All-kenning eye of Oðin used primarily in all artes involving navigation. Even when the Sun remains hidden, the gift of Fore-sight in its arteful use is One-eye's gift from Wisdom's own Bright Well.

His 'sun-eye' is therefore most probably the right eye, governing the active and forthright kennings. This gift of Fore-sight, acquired by hanging on the Tree (see Havamal) in suspension from the bough of Mim/ir, releases the dewy elixir. As another cultural exemplar and avatar of Chronus and Cain, Oðin becomes the reaper of souls, dispatcher unto death and psychopompic guide for all souls to Asgardhr, thereto remain to fight again at Ragnorak. Or to Hela, where in Nifleheimr they will find their way into Her Great Cauldron: 'Hvergelmir.' Here souls are first washed in the Lethe and returned to the realm of man.

Wisdom is ever the ultimate prize. The Sagas sing of its Virtue and Gnosis, of how hard the trial is for the winning of it, and how only the legends whisper their secrets, of mysteries intrinsically linked to this sacred tree. By succour of root and stem will the 'mead,' the virtue of knowledge, of life and death be shared. The relationship betwixt tree, well and cup can never be overstated. Subject then unto Fate and Time, Oðin feared greatly the loss of Huginn, of Mind, primarily of 'Fore-thought' the gift of prophecy, of clear sight in eternity. But, he feared still, and no less, the

119

loss of Muginn, of Memory and Hind-sight, within Time, an equally precious gift. Yet still, Oðin sought the wits of eloquence and of poetry, pooled from within the Great Well of Mim/ir. Perhaps it should therefore be offered for consideration, the possibility that Oðin's 'sight' sacrificed to Mim/ir (The 'Head' and Over Well of Mind) for Wisdom's blinding, was that of both eyes, feign always to illusion and deception. He'd acquired the *faculty* to attain Fore-sight, the intuitive virtue to always 'know,' to 'see' what is 'Fated' ahead in Eternity. Balanced by Memory, the Mindfulness of Hind-sight, Wisdom is devoid of intuition. Mim/ir knew that only in their combined faculties, would Fate and Time, imbue Truth, the Wisdom of the Sages. His sacrifice then, was to 'lose sight' of all that existed in the limited vision of his left and right eyes. Combined, they synthesised the third, that of true wisdom, the cyclopean eye of myth and legend, known from Asia to the Mediterranean, and from the Urals to the Pyrenees. Only this single eye was beyond forgetfulness, beyond ignorance, beyond Time and beyond Fate.

The price for this precious oracle was ever in Oðin's aegis, and in its surrender was a gift for humankind to attain; Oðin needed only to impart its virtue. Mim/ir now guards the Clarity of Truth, for the future to come, for all time. Many speak also of the head of Mim/ir, of myths wherein all honourable regard is given in homage to that very 'head,' consulted oft by Oðin, seeking its virtue of clarity. Having sacrificed and gained all She had gifted to Him, 'Hind-sight,' the mark of the Gods upon Time and upon humanity, remains within the eternal now, the ever-present and ever changing moment as the bridge and kinetic *point* of flux towards Fore-sight, of prophecy. Hence, in all urgency, Oðin now shifts between the 'quick and the dead,' across the Lethe, travelling between the worlds, riding Sleipnir to greet each dawn at the well of Urdhr. Urdhr's Well, is conversely that which exists 'beneath' (the Clouds), it is the 'Under'

World Well of All, reflecting the continuity of life, as the constancy of each moment through the ability of every bead of that elixir to retain the 'memory of all things.'

Oðin's single eye, not fallen to that Well, carries with Him all He sees there; the memory and burden of the past, bringing it always into the 'now,' through the Hind-sight of reflected wisdom, as the Eternal Now, into Fore-sight—the Gift of Truth and Wisdom. Had He left memory behind, there could be no future. Had He left the wherewithal to think astutely, only stasis would ensue. Without knowledge of our past, who and what we are, we are as dead things. We wither, uncertain of direction and purpose.

> "*Mind and Heart*
> *make their flight every day*
> *over the limitless land.*
> *For Mind I fear*
> *he may not come back,*
> *though I am more anxious for*
> *Heart.*"[34]

Always, the imperative remains secure in the Tide of Life. In the eternal Tide of Hypnos and Thanatos, Oðin drifts to each Well, to focus ahead with clear vision: with gnosis. If lacking clarity there, how could He foretell when Ragnarok will occur, the hinge-pin of Lore and Law to most northern Clans and Tribes. How otherwise to view the whole world, even in sleep? And of the Mysteries of His Eye: V/alfather's pledge: Oðin's mead, flowing forever, a pledge to humanity given to the water-spirit Mim/ir (or Mim), an exchange of sight/of wisdom in all realms, past and future, that it might always exist in the present, a gift of the gods to those whom they favour. And thus all things become known to us through memory from within Urdhr's well and through intuition drawn from Mim/ir's well. Mim/ir 'drinks the magic mead from a horn' which is then used to pour water onto the great ash Yggdrasil.

Again, in another tale Oðin wanders in all manner of disguise to secure the eternal flow of wisdom into the realm of Midgardhr. Wherever there is 'mead' horded, Oðin conceives a way to release it; paying duty to Mim/ir, in gyfu obligation. Mim/ir's Well is the mirror between the heaven and the earth, the one Bowers refers to as 'the third' (mirror) and the macro/microcosmic eye.

> *"Compassion is a cover for the ruthlessness of total truth. Truth is another name for godhead." Her "works are good but also black with works of darkness, yet both are compassionate."*[135]

Only Her wisdom (She), through fore-knowledge then may loosen those 'bonds,' remove their restrictions, facilitating attainment of all seals needed to pass through, recognised as kin. Only Fate, fuelled by Truth, shatters the fetters of illusion, of time, of life, of being, of all that never was.

> *"Every bond I loosed from you, every chain from the underworld I broke, these things bound upon my people, detaining them. These high walls of darkness I overthrew, and those gates, barred by they who lack compassion, locked by the pitiless ones; those I broke, and shattered"*[136]

Through compassion, the gods determined that Eve in gnostic legend, should birth a daughter, named Norea—Wisdom's own reflection into manifestation. Norea and Her spouse (Seth) are then established as manifest avatars and tutelary spirits (though not ours), but having a similar presence and parallel historical significance. Norea represents a saviour-figure to be exonerated through the cherishment and adoration of humanity. Their love for Her, elevates them all. This principle, though much changed in culture, is perhaps another discreet nod to the older, more obscure traditions absorbed by Candlemas, retained by the Clan.

The relevant gnostic text describes the calling to Her (by Her two names), stood upon the Four Luminaries (the Four Lights) to intercede for Her. These may refer to the Four Angels of the 'Face/Presence,' the Throne Angels. Heralded at this time within The Covenanted Rite, Bowers was sensitive to the importance of that particular symbology, having perennial importance to all faiths layered as they are through variant cultures, each finding relevance through unique expression. We maintain four similar quarter-men, poised around the Maid, holding aloft their lanterns, during the mystery of the unveiling of the 'Childe of Promise.'

Gnostic myths and forms have naturally morphed in varying degrees over time. Furthermore, once subject to those traditions, they were easily absorbed. Several forms of Her name are known, including Na'amah, whose task is to awaken those dedicated to Her, to remind them of the work they need to undertake to go 'Home,' (again). What begins to transpire here is a rising recognition, a stirring familiarity, a knowing.

"For She will gather them home again."[137]

Gateways between realms are held by guides who observe wouldbe travellers. Ever alert, they sense the lack of preparation exhibited by those who would traverse to those regions, who are, all too often, far too ill-prepared to cross effectively. Five material bonds, five elemental maxims forge the gateways that stand between stasis and evolution. Five are the elements that anneal the soul in the great work, five here, in Hela's abode, and seven above, in the arc of the Celestial 'Heavens.' Our 'bonds' are no more, and no less than our deeds. Our 'bonds' are our oaths. Our bonds are our words, spoken as vows, and as prayer and incantation. These five attainments guard the realms between each gate and the next. Virtues gleaned from them find some recognition as the five material elements made flesh, made word, deed and action. They are named for: Fate, Time, Ignorance, Oblivion and Forgetfulness.

Here upon this plane of life, of trial, of endeavour, vigour and will, this Middle-earth is the midway garden home—Midgardhr. Here we gather all the memories and wisdoms needed to live a good life and to die a good death; fated to move on, to dine awhile with the gods, fight the sweeping demands of chaos, then enjoy anew the throes of bliss, evermore. Though no explicit rite is 'known' of exoterically to break the five seals, it is 'known' esoterically as the *Pentamychos*, the 'Five chambers of the Heart', the hero's quest and destiny of the warrior priest, where folklore fuses romance and legend to hold forever in memory all deeds and beliefs of these ancestral giants. Sigilised upon the Shield, Gawain's Pentagram, symbolised the Rose garden fable; expressed through the Round of Life. Protennoia, as guide, mentor and divine instructress, becomes the saviour of the elect. Bowers refers to Her intensely as the divine Muse—She who is All Destiny.[138] Through Her gifts will the signs and symbols be known. Their sounds will reveal the names of the guides who guide the way.

> "*During the persecution the adherents of the Mystery system went underground and joined forces with the aboriginal beliefs of the masses, and so became part of traditional witchcraft. Centuries passed and the meaning behind much ritual was forgotten, or relegated to a superstitious observance to elemental Nature. Much of the old ritual that has survived became ossified and repeated by rote, rather than by understanding. Consequently, it has become static and remote from its original purpose, which was to enlighten the follower spiritually.*"[139]

She instructs the way of silence, the value of creation from silence and repose, ensuring that; "*These, will by no means taste death.*"[140]

Rather than pray, invoke, contemplate and petition the gods through the body, which is 'outside,' she declares we must open ourselves through spirit, which is 'inside':

> *"It is therefore fitting to pray to the father and to call on him with all our soul—not externally with the lips, but with the spirit, which is inward, which came forth from the depth—sighing"*[141]

The One exists 'in Silence.' That is the silence of its own vibration, a primal sound, uttered by the inner spirit, reverberating out of itself. Thusly, *Tri-morphic Protennoia* gifts a Trinity of Language formulated as: the Voice (Father), the Sound (Mother) and the Word (Son). This incredibly profound Truth finds emotive expression within the 'Mask' Prayer, specifically the end, in the blessing of the Clan doxology.

> *"In the name of the All father, the dark and bright twins, and the Three Mothers, whose Spirit Moves All."*

Sophia Prounicos, we may recall, as the serpent of the tree, is the voice of the Father (*'I am the light of thought'*), the speech of the Mother (*'I am the expression of thought'*) and the word of the Christos (*'I am the unification and assimilation of both voice and speech,'* given as the revelation of the One Truth—*Vac*). In terms of the Trinity, Her virtue is expressed through the Word that is Her voice. The manifestation of breath is particularly clear when speaking certain vowels sequences, the hidden names are therein glorified. The Gnostic language preserves the greatest Mystery through sacred silence.

Ignorance of fate and of the wit to overcome it is a fearful state. Hence, as we share in the Houzle, we abjure such fate, declaring it partaken with: *"Girt terror and fearful dread."* To celebrate this glorious existence, in that Round of Life, we must remain mindful as we each partake of the Houzle to include the three elements that reflect triune divinity. Wine, bread and salt: we must remain mindful too, how Salt is:

"A reminder of man's labour and his worth."[142]

Other traditions have likewise held salt in equal esteem: *Leviticus* 2:13 demands that all offerings should include a grain of salt for Asherah. In the Gospel of Philip, a Gnostic variation offers explanation of how Sophia is the salt present in the Eucharist; without salt, the offering is deemed void, unworthy, thereafter:

'The Hound will turn his nose up at the cake.'[143]

The hierarchy of sounds resonates sacred names, and so required the development of a series of 'diphthongs' to disguise them from those untrained to their distinctions. As elongated vowels, they allow creation and insertion of superior intermediate 'vowels.'

The seven II. I. E. U. O. A. AA: *"sacred vowels of witchcraft…become the name of the sun king…the vowels are the sacred tree sequence of the north, which amount to the mysteries of witchcraft as opposed to paganism."*[144] In the ancient world, Greek and Egyptians had recorded their usage of seven sacred vowels: *ayy, eee, ahh, iii, oohh, uuu, oow;* (the five diphthongs are: ai, au, ei, eu, ou,) *"And the throne of his glory was established (...) on which his un-revealable name is inscribed, on the tablet [...] the word, the Father of the light of everything, he who came forth from the silence."*[145] The pneumatic 'Spirit' as breath, is totally coterminous with the sacred Penta-grammaton: *Yod—Heh-Shin-Vau—Heh*, The Round of Life: Birth: Youth/Love: Maturity/Maternity, Wisdom and Death, central to the Mythos of 'Cochrane's Clan,' and thus by default, ours, as heirs to that tradition. They relate directly to the 'mystical' precepts listed by Bowers in his paper entitled: 'The Faith of the Wise' where he instructs how:

"Devotion requires proof. Therefore, that proof exists within the disciplines of the Faith. The nature of proof cannot be explained, since force can only be

shown by inference and by participation, not by intellectual reasoning. The nature of the proof falls into many forms, but amongst the most common are these:

(a) POETIC VISION, in which the participant has inward access to dream images and symbols. This is the result of the unconscious being stimulated by various means. Images are taught as part of a tradition, and also exist.(as Jung speculated) upon their own levels. They are, when interpreted properly, means by which a lesser part of truth may be understood.

(b) THE VISION OF MEMORY, in which the devotee not only remembers past existence but also, at times, a past perfection.

(c) MAGICAL VISION, in which the participant undertakes by inference part of a Triad of service, and therefore contacts certain levels.*

(d) RELIGIOUS VISION, in which the worshipper is allowed admission to the True Godhead for a short time. This is a part of true initiation, and the results of devotion towards a mystical aim.

(e) MYSTICAL VISION, in which the servant enters into divine union with the Godhead. This state has no form, being a point where force alone is present.

These are proofs, since having enjoined with such forces, there cannot afterwards be any doubts as to the nature of the experience. Man suffers from doubt at all times, but to the participant in such experience, the doubt centres around the reality of the external world, not the inner. The reality of such experience illuminates the whole life. Therefore it can be shown that the Faith is a complex philosophy, dealing finally with the nature of Truth, Experience and Devotion. It requires discipline and work; plus utter and complete devotion to the common aim.

It can only be fulfilled by service, some labours taking many years to complete.

The Faith tolerates no nonsense, and those who would come to it, must come empty-handed saying "I know nothing, I seek everything," since within the structure of the Faith, all things may be contained and are contained.

It has survived, in secrecy and silence, the attacks of persecution, indifference and misrepresentation. It is secret because those only who are best suited may enter the awful silences of the Places of the Gods. It is silent because in silence there is strength, protection and a future. It is also silent today, because as the Greeks said:

"Those whom the Gods would destroy, they first make mad."

It is nearly impossible to enter unless the supplicant shows unmistakable signs of past memory and a genuine mystical drive, and is willing to undertake tests that will force him finally to disclose that matter which is most secret to himself. The Faith has no secrets in the sense that there are formulas which can be readily understood and taught. It is finally and utterly the True Faith, standing immovable beyond space, time and all human matters.

*Being requested by the Editor to clarify this statement I ask the interested reader to examine the Hebrew letters IHV as they would be in their original and matriarchal form, which will explain something of the basic nature of magical rite and ritual. It should be as clear as the Roebuck in the Thicket now."[146]

This Pentagrammatic glyph is a microcosm of the *'glory'* or *'splendour'* of Creation; this finds further expression through five stages of virtue, as a lived testament to the Covenant named above. These vital core principles, so treasured by Bowers, are keys to a spiritual and mystical pathway towards Truth, that became the seal upon which the 'real' Cochrane Tradition is predicated. From Clan studies of this 'Round of Life,' the following may be added as our understanding of it.

1   **Poetic Vision**—stimulation through imagery of traditional symbols that generate intuitive perception in dreams and trance work (use of logic or reason considered an obstruction to this process).

2   **Vision of Memory**—process of anamnesis, of former levels of existence and the harvesting of gnosis achieved from them.

3   **Magical Vision**—immersion and envelopment of Kabbalistic principles; primarily, this would necessitate working with the Three (Hebraic) Mothers (Aleph, Mem and Shin) via the Three Rings of the Moat. The purpose is Seer-ship, Oracular Questing and Thaumaturgy. The Norns/Fates. The Tree: Midgardhr; Utgardhr and Asgardhr.

4   **Religious Vision**—part of a true 'Initiation'; the mystical aim of the Vigil. Temporary access of devotee to godhead. Wherein the Cosmology of the Mythos is realised.

5   **Mystical Vision**—in which the servant (a pilgrim, who in full humility, surrenders themselves), rather than the devotee enters full union with Godhead. In this, awareness of form ceases; there exists the point of force alone – *'fanaa,'* the annihilation of ego. Merkavah. Eschatology of the Mythos.

Cumulatively, these demonstrate the evolution of: perception, gnosis, seer-ship, vigil (challenge/trial/surrender) and union. (Individuation) They also relate to the round of live: *birth, youth, love, wisdom, death*

a	1	birth	mercury	Think/memory	yod	seed
e	2	youth	apollo	See/magical	heh	sprout
i	3	love	saturn	Hear/religious	shin	flower
o	4	wisdom	jupiter	Know/poetic	vau	seed
u	5	death	venus	Feel/mystical	heh	stasis

$15 = 6$; so as each sense is five times five (25) then the hexagram becomes the pentagram. In this 'Round of Life' (as chartered in table above) we may note the five points of fellowship, the handshake of gyfu —the troth between 'both as one.'

We may finally return to those sacred numbers, 49 and 12. Jovially, Bowers remarks to Bill Gray[147] that he will not be shooting an arrow through a Garland at *49 paces on 12th* Night without further qualification. Clearly he expected Bill Gray to fully understand his intent; they shared a basis in the aforementioned gnostic theology and equally, of heathen lore, sufficient for them to hint obliquely to that lore, and yet be confident they are each fully conversant of the other's intent. All five of these profound expressions are intrinsic to the Mythos, teachings and praxes of the Clan of Tubal Cain that serve to remove all doubt, except upon the veracity thereafter of the so-called 'external' world.

'All realities become True at some level.
All realities become possible to experience.
Inner illumination reifies the outer form of being.'

Returning to the issue of secrecy, Roy Bowers in contemplation of this vital Pentalphic formulae, emphasised how the only secret regarding these five proofs, is that which makes one able to enter the silent realms of the gods. Such an enigma, is beyond expression. It is a paradox not taught by human contact. It is the virtue of 'the blood'—that which he 'holds,'[148] but does not own, and that which is gifted to him but may not give. Of this, he said:

"If I call upon my ancestors, I call upon forces that are within myself and exterior, now you know what I mean, when I speak of the burden of Time."[149]

Tragically, his star rose and fell, burning fiercely, leaving his work unfinished; even this he had predicted.

"I keep on getting the feeling that we are preparing the groundwork for a crop that we will not reap, waiting for a dawn that may never come, but wait we must. We are the force for something else that is to occur, the creators of opinion for a new concept that is arising somewhere in the world." [150]

Nike the Conqueror, Nike the beautiful, Victorious, the Peacemaker; She who gave Prometheus the gift of Fire, who in turn gave this to humankind at Her behest. With remarkable intuitive foresight, Bowers recognised the innovative cataclysmic dynamic of the virtue invoked through the Egregore of the Clan's tutelary deity—Tubal Cain. Nonetheless, in just a short a time, a mere eight years; he had found and lost everything. Here he had glimpsed the Grail, but felt unworthy to take it. In that single flash of self-realisation, he witnessed again the awesome presence of Truth that had so haunted him, since first She embraced him, rousing him to Her banner as Pale Guiden. In deference to that banner, he adhered to its 'Law.'

Eternal ring of Fate, we weave the Ouroboros wreath of the unmanifest within the manifest; we weave the dead within the living; we weave our fears within our hopes and we weave love into being, that life will ever be the Source, the beginning and the end of all things; in fate and better so. Alpha Omega

♦ The Gordian Knot: Kairos

"The authority of time manifest within eternity as the Law"—the fourth nail and axis of the 'eternal now' grounds equilibrium at source. On the magickal usage of 'Cords,' Roy Bowers had much to say about their use and purpose. But do we, today consider them in the same way? Has our world-view changed our perception of the 'witch's ladder'? To what practical purpose does it serve, still? It seems increasingly unlikely that Fate, as a Virtue is held today with like esteem to that of our ancestors. In terms of the

'Gordian Knot' and its inherent symbolism regarding the ciphers of gnosis imbued within it by a lineage of priest-kings, it is tempting to assume hubris invited their doom, whence Alexander failed to recognise the true purpose within the knot's onerous binding.

Once we cease to understand the meaning of a thing, and fail to recognise the purpose it serves, how does its continued application serve us, in any reality? Where in this transposition does true magick reign? In the operative fulfilment of duty, we follow Fate's dictates to assume the mantle of our destiny, yet we buck all challenges with an indignant force of will. Which choice effectively cheats fate and which truly overcomes it?

Another way to describe Kairos, is: True Will (Greek Thelema). There is a True Will within each of us, our Destiny, so to speak. If we can determine what we truly want and line our life up with that, nothing is impossible. Each of us is created with a True Will, a true purpose, a Destiny; it is the action of aligning mind with heart, and thus with Destiny. An historical example explores Alexander the king, in his resonant mythic role as both hero and anti-hero. Greek myths are adversarial in nature, opting for devil's advocate in their unsubtle manner of obliging each of us to act in accordance with True Will—Thelema. That is, they resist advice on how to live, but offer instead consideration on how NOT to live.

That is, paying attention to causality. Oedipus is an exemplar of that statute. Alexander's brazen flouting of the Parcae's prime directive is another. In cutting the Gordian knot, Alexander's aggressive act failed to eliminate the challenge, with or without the realisation of the Fate he unleashed, automatically, by nature of its release? Concerning the ruminations on Fate, Providence, Destiny and Wyrd, can we really cheat Fate by submitting to the Will of Hekate? Evan John Jones suggests we may, by *unbinding* Her knots in a manner contra to Alexander's hubris who severed his own fateful (Gordian) knot. Despite the choices offered at each juncture and crossroads, we can only ever act according to Wyrd, that is to say, the choice we make will be the right one for that moment; it could never be otherwise.

Retrospectively we may feel it could have been different, but that first instinctive choice is that in complete accord within Wyrd at that given moment. Certain aspects of Fate are certain and inviolable. Though, if one had total awareness perhaps then one could cut through the Gordian Knot for one would be free of Fate, but who may claim that? Perhaps Alexander's undoing does reside in his unmistakable hubris, but maybe that was Fated too? As we are born to die, it stands to reason that he who follows fate without awareness, does so as an automaton, making mechanical gestures that articulate only the calculated 'mean' response, opposed to the less considered and intuitive, yet needful prompt.

> *"Alexander the Great, by cutting the Gordian knot, announced to all and sundry that he was going to cut his own fate with the edge of a sword. It was the action of a truly brave man, since the knot was bound upon the Twins Bulls, the Masters over Life and Death. It may be that when he built a temple to Nemesis, he was attempting to buy off the terrible fate of his former action.*"[151]

Alexander achieved 'god-like' status, but only that comparable to the method by which he tackled the knot of Fate. In his world, one lived and died by the sword. If he had released Fate by alternate means, would he have achieved a greater spiritual apotheosis? Of course, Alexander could have chosen to simply leave the knot intact, bypass it, ignore it, but at what price? The Oracle had foretold that only he who defeated its challenge would rule the whole of Asia. Ambitious and bold, Alexander could not afford to fail; one way or another, the problem demanded solving. So, the question of whether he was acting in accordance to his prescribed destiny, would always be, yes, naturally, as this is subject to pre-destination (but it is imperative here to not confuse this with pre-determined). The better question would ask: In cutting the knot, was Alexander overcoming his Fate, or entangled within it?

Choice is the gift of Fate, it is all we have to accelerate or inhibit our smooth transport through life towards our ultimate destiny as individuals and as humankind. This also reflects the journey as the individual within the collective typified most particularly in the gnostic faith, of pilgrim wanderer touching upon the lives of others, sharing them, then moving ever-closer to their own goal. Fate itself hangs above

OUROBOROS

each and every one of us as the Sword of Damocles, serving to remind us of the burden of choice and the means to operate it. In wielding that sword, Alexander took control of his fate; his will determined that outcome. Is this really the same as 'being in fate' in order to overcome it? In hubris, did he mistake destiny for role, and fate for will? Certainly, he fulfilled the prophecy, but again, was that 'his' by right, or by the force of might he exacted to secure it?

Only the individual would truly know if they had acted thus. No history or analysis could comprehend the journey of the soul of another; we follow only the manifest actions, we may not be privy to that inner journey of torment and despair, but also of elation and rapture. Approaching the dynamic of the Hero raises a complex dilemma of how we embrace Wyrd, of how we act when placed upon that fateful moment on the crossroads, each, and every day. Many of these decisions appear trivial, yet their consequences are incalculable. Others appear insurmountable, yet by instinct and intuition are 'overcome; almost effortlessly, and yet the demands may be 'fatal.'

♦ What makes a person into a Hero?

There are of course many reasons and as many causes. However, one above the numerous common motives is that of selflessness in the face of adversity, or the offering of the one for the many, wherein the greater good is served. Effectively this generates the survival of 'Hope' where the best of us return again as carnate beings into a world decimated by the ills, woes and chaos released by Pandora, a world peopled by egotists and the self-serving. We must therefore approach the hero's journey as one undertaken by the individual, as the returning avatar, bearing equal relevance to the collective he serves, whose endurance sets the context for his/her/their return? Myth, legend and history abound with such figures, whose presence, albeit brief leaves a mark that anchors our evolution to an ideal, a 'bright beacon' in the fog perhaps?

Two clichés perfectly pronounce how, 'It is always darkest before the dawn' and that 'hope springs eternal': such is the triumphant premise of 'the rightness of order,' of the restoration of cosmic law manifest within, and upon the continuity of our species. Ever the jester's weapon, the historical wit and noble arte of 'punning,' was a blade in the Saxon and Norse armoury, in verse and prose, written and oral. In more ancient praxis, this scoping arte had been the preserve of mystery schools, where irony, rhetoric, polemic, and satire were intrinsic to the journey towards understanding the mystery of the word, of the secrets within, and of the power conveyed by it. The pen is ever mightier than the sword (though clearly not for Alexander), having significance worthy of its demography of chaos. Taking the hero's journey into such realms, where every subtle nuance of a known and perceived reality is brutally challenged. Roy Bowers said:

"In certain states of hyper-suggestion, the human mind can and does create anything it sees fit as its own personal reality. The only difference between the visionary and the schizophrenic is the emotional state."[152]

Hence, much has been spoken of the 'force' of perception, but little of the 'forms' by which it clothes itself. Again, Roy Bowers said of this:

"Nothing is so unreal than the reality that surrounds us...reality is the better word for the other planes, they are all force..." [153]

All things being equal, does the hero's journey cut across all planes of reality simultaneously or consecutively, or even randomly (assuming of course that random is an accepted directive within Fate) and in each case, is there a subtle determinative anchor for a prescribed 'sense' of reality? In other words, do we properly exercise that all-important 'emotional state' once faced with the reality of our gifts? Perhaps if we attempt to bridge this apparent dichotomy with the perspective Bowers posits exists between 'the emotional state' and 'desire,' we may discern its elusive principle. He believed most ardently how desire drives the poet, artist or philosopher to explore alternative realms of reality with the express purpose of experiencing it/them, via a 'willed' connection. To that end, their work focuses upon the object of that desire, rather than themselves. Symbols especially are comprehended through inspiration; focussed upon with intent and acted upon with purpose, they present the only relevant 'reality' requisite to 'the work.' Of course, Roy Bowers laid great import on symbols, their use and their evolution.

As a statement, the *"higher purpose within divine reality,"* assumes without conflict our own intention, though perhaps one that finds better expression as an indistinct state, awaiting only one's awareness to engage it meaningfully for that purpose. The initial pun—'define/divine' as a prescriptive of origin, serves to relay a perspective of reality as something indefinable as an absolute. Present in all modes of experience and comprehension, it is a subtle state claimed by Bowers as an exponential shift induced by 'desire' (emotion), chosen by the intentional challenge of the individual's boundaries of perception, rather than restrictions imposed by them. Contra to this, certain alternatives modes of understanding such as schizophrenia, invoke an uncomfortable shift in all those perceptions for what constitutes as subjective and objective 'reality.' Our challenge to understand their subtleties is teased via the enigmatic maxim:

"In fate and the overcoming of fate lies the grail."

To paraphrase Roy Bowers, who presents the caveat here, that it is better by far to envision ALL realms of reality, wherein all causalities are

noted and a path chartered directly towards the *object* of 'desire,' minus
ALL distraction that could hinder its success. To rely on angels to catch
us err we fall, induces the element of fear, now introduced: fools enter
only where angels fear to tread. Adrenalin fuels and is fuelled by such
intrepid awe. Giving rise to the primal incentive of: fight or flight, it is
indeed an adverse emotion that feeds the beast. Too easy is the fall to
false discernment; too easy to assume corruption and laxity among the
gods. Again, here is another thorn that sorely troubled Roy Bowers, one
evinced most profoundly through his emphasis on 'Faith.' For if we
abandon our gods, rather than seeking Truth, as that which resides beyond
them (yet discovered in apprehension of them), would we not be guilty
of feeding that beast even more.

♦ Same Fate, different destiny?

Freedom is a state of mind, which, through life and fate we attempt to
bring to actuation. For despite apparent adversity and chaos, we choose
our responses. What we may not choose for ourselves, are the
circumstances of imposed prisons, borne of external events and
influences. Upon those forces, we have no point of resistance; need fuels
the primal instinct, where all too often, our ego-driven desire overrides
its dictates. Were we to 'know' our Fate, then, in running with it, rather
than against it, we would be equipped to overcome it. Succumbing to
desire is that 'fateful' choice, and its repeated management presses home
the requisite of grasping what is 'needful.'

The Law, states: '*do what is necessary, not what you desire*' Stepping back
into analysis negates the instinctive connection that severs true need, the
same 'need' that facilitates the act of enforcing 'not what we desire, but
what is necessary.' Perhaps Alexander, 'knew' this to be the truest sense,
and acted accordingly, accepting and embracing his Fate, for the realisation
of his Destiny inculcated by it? Had he withdrawn from such drama,

would that great destiny have remained in his path to claim? Not ultimately perhaps, but certainly in that incarnation. Roy Bowers might opine that in seizing Fate actively is to 'act within Fate,' gifting freedom from this round of life, working thereafter towards our attainment of the 'grail.'

Wyrd is the manifold 'Virtue of Fate,' actuated in pursuit of one's destiny, wherein Providence is key. Recognition of these symbols today is as relevant as they were 2300 years ago. Each knot is a maze, a step upon the tiered pillar of reversal, where all heroes are fated to die, where great deeds are generated by the appearance of the breaking of a 'sacred taboo'—in this case the severing rather than the untying of the knot. To them is given the task of unleashing holy fire, chaos and distraction— needful challenges, needful work. Indeed the Hero wears a thousand faces—all Hers. Prophecy has no limit. Yet to fulfil the prophecy, Alexander, like so many before and since, clearly acted correctly, as the vessel of change, he instigated missive anarchy and flux. Had he chosen to act contra to this given mission, then Fate would have needed to find another agent by whom the spear point may ignite the waters within the great cauldron, perpetuating the swirlings that maintain the crucial balance between order and chaos, life and death.

6
The
Hearth

'Magical subtlety is about inference rather than obfuscation in a world where things are not always as they seem.'

Between hearth, and hearth-stone, lies a huge grotto of mythopoeia; traversed through lore, and by virtue of visionary inspiration, caution towards seeming or assumed commonalities, should, in all wisdom find adoption as the 'basis' for fire. Central to life's purpose, domestic or esoteric, our ancestors found comfort in its portability. Far too often overlooked are the mutable and shifting patterns of settlement, acquired slowly, cumulatively, as generations of nomadic life adopted the yoke of the land, of farmsteads and livestock. Amongst nomadic lifestyles, the hearth had been the historic focus of folk, gathered about the area used for cooking and eating. It later gained distinction as the hearth-stone, symbolising settlement, the establishment and ownership of land and of the community buildings that encompassed it. The former is centred upon Suzerainty, the latter in Sovereignty; both determine with utmost relevance, the form and function of any people aligned to either. Adjunct to this, we must deliberate how fire, around which all peoples sit, eat, dance, pray, sing, tell stories, as the hub and heart of that society, is able to generate such intrinsic distinction; and yet, it does precisely that. If a people 'move and shift with time and tide,' we may deduce their Egregore is carried within that fire and the hearth of its making, however temporary, to secure warmth, succour, light and most importantly, the centralising cosmology for those people. Spirit answers the call, summoned through and in answer to the calling. Stronger is this, where the People are one.

Nonetheless, a 'Hearth' is always the hub and heart of a people. Mobile or intransient, it is always the life of a community. If laid for permanency, then the Hearth-stone binds those *people to that place* in addition to each other. The other, erected temporarily as a portable Hearth, binds its people to that significance.

Neither of these suggest superiority over the other and neither exclude the invocation of tutelary spirits, ancestral shades, presence of phenomenon etc. Both generate connections to the 'other.' The veil of mystery fascinates in the truest sense of that 'Word,' and any explanation of intellect is bound to suffer in translation. Within earlier Palaeolithic societies, recumbent stones deemed to be Her body, personified the earthen altar in the fullest sense.

These continue to serve as the central focus of many dwellings as hearthstones. Charged within the 'Old Covenant,' the Maid as 'bride' of the Old Horn King is represented by the Hearthstone, binding Her spirit with His to the Stang She holds, transmuting its Virtue to Her Clan, a co-hesive unit for its survival and continuity. In this manner, the 'House that Jack Built' becomes through the son/sun, embodied within the figure of the Maid as refuge for the Egregoric spirit.[154] All past and present members of the People weave together their spiritual energies to generate and sustain the Egregore—even after death. As it is the soul that shifts into re-birth with memory, within its mind soul, that spirit mind of the Clan remains with the *'quick and the dead'* as we become *one* in truth. Those beyond the Clan, the Castle, Egregore and Shield, though unable to access or tap into the spirit-mind of the Clan, may access or sense, perhaps even connect with the mind-soul of extant members, and possibly with memory traces only, of past members of the Clan until their re-return, home again. Earth to earth and ashes to ashes—blood to bone, flesh to ground, and life to the hearth, one more renewed. This is very different for ourselves, as we 'of' the Clan, access both, before and after, in all stages and beyond.

"The Egregore is the link, the key, the heart and mind of the Clan..."

and also:

"The hearth, the altar the stang are one and the same—the hunter, the hunted and old tubal are but one."

John (E.J.J.) asserted that:

"The Clan 'is' where the Stang rests"[155]

Imagine then a triad: a soul (Maid), a mind (Robin), and spirit (the Egregore). Bound as *one*, as a fused synergy through, and of the Stang, which at its simplest, is the corporeal element where these potencies manifest, as both a visual and physical symbol of the Clan, bearing the authority and presence of our tutelary deities in the north. Robin refers to the 'Appointment of Office' as validated by the Stang, to those without the Clan, but it also bears significance to those bound to its aegis, within the Clan. If lost or stolen, this ancestral totemic artefact would become an erstwhile prize in lieu of its wondrous and most sacred status; a symbol only of its true and actual virtue, in form and force. Beyond that, devoid of the key, the vehicle is useless to them. The Merkabah shifts only when we come together as ONE. Again, this is precisely why John (E.J.J) held 'guard' for the Clan, awaiting the presence of Virtue (the soul key), to activate the Stang he guarded, but did not 'hold,' in the absolute sense. He made note of this task within his books, that, as caretaker of that legacy, it was never his gift. He remains a true knight of the Grail.

It behoves us to add, how the surrender of ourselves in eternal service to the People, its memories and its Fate, as the Word and Deed, coalesces that potent causality John (E.J.J.) states unequivocally as 'Hers' already—the Virtue of the Clan to whom all are bound. All owe their absolute obligation to the Maid and unwavering duty to the Magister. As luminescent qutub, the Stang, described by Bowers in his letters, is composed of three parts, of female and male, forming the divine hermaphrodite at the crux. 'Context' reveals everything it is said, and the primal gods of the archaic world are herein presented, preserving the cosmology of the 'Clan of Tubal Cain' and its eschatology, inviting true seekers to walk again in Eden. How we achieve that sublime destiny, is a task that focuses upon the Stang as a pivotal key. The Staff or Stang is a Holy Tree expressed pointedly as the 'mark' of sacrifice, in both deed and principle. Numerous religious analogies and mythological allegories, share, in prose and verse, the fundamental tenet of willing surrender by the male hero/priest/king to the 'Tree' of life/death/wisdom. Essentially, the Stang is the perfumed altar, the active point of sacrifice as the iconic embodiment of the Clan's triune deity.

> *"Throughout the history of humanity, there have been myths, schools of wisdom and teachers, who have shown a way to attain a working knowledge of esoteric thought and philosophy by using inference rather than direct method, to teach the approaches to cosmic truth. The secrecy of these Masters has nothing to do with protecting the Mysteries, since all that can be said about the Mysteries has already been written into folklore, myth and legend.*
>
> *What is not forthcoming is the explanation. It was recognised that these legends, rituals and myths were the roads through many layers of consciousness to the area of the mind where the soul can exist in its totality. These and their surrounding disciplines and teachings became what the West describes as the Mysteries. The Mysteries are, in essence, means by which man may perceive his own inherent divinity."*[156]

◆ Kith and Kin

Kneeling before anyone to acknowledge the divine essence they may hold with true Virtue; is respectful, a manifest honour shared. Kneeling before the divine to surrender all that is human within the self, acknowledges the divine within oneself: this is to honour our existence within the All. Of the many who speak of the divine, too few of them uphold such humility that is equally a process of integrity. Honour and pride have been replaced by status and esteem.

Therefore, once we have a need to speak of supposed commonalities of tradition, these must of necessity, remain distinct. We may delight in those things we share, yet still, must respect and retain the points of divergence. With regard to exclusivity, any authentic holder of Virtue need not be concerned by competing factions, because claim what they will, spirit serves its own and will not work through them. Kith and Kin of course remain intrinsically linked. Our kin is held dear, as is all kith. From all modalities, do pilgrims share the road ahead. From within, and of this stream, elements of essential alchemy process all form, whether approached singularly or in Companie. By any means necessary, we acquire self-gnosis and an altered perspective of the path before us, the better to pay that forward for the benefit of our community, of our kin.

Defined as a fusion of psycho-spiritual and magickal symbols within philosophical enquiry, egress is facilitated via cumulative personal epiphanies and fateful occurrence. Those who enter a stream of any Mystery Tradition must first be aware of the capacity in which they seek its activation. Understanding is everything. Nothing begets nothing; hence it is deemed, beyond all else, 'The Great Work.' To claim otherwise, denotes a failure to apprehend its enormity, and makes fact of that folly!

"The Faith is finally concerned with Truth, total Truth. It is one of the oldest

of religions, and also one of the most potent, bringing as it does, Man into contact with Gods, and Man into contact with Self." [157]

♦ Faith

Words and language depend entirely upon context and semantic shifts that occur throughout its long history. Oblique features are extrapolated during experiential encounters within the Mysteries proper, especially via the metaphysical ranks of certain Gnostics and Neo-Platonists, in whose loquacious references we discover the uncertainty of being, described as reflections of Sophia—the Greek logos. The Word expresses the manifestation of thought, and thought can be guided, molded, manipulated and precipitated.

An inspired mentor will fashion ideas as if the thought had been ever present, which of course it had. Anamnesis requires only the essential catalyst to awaken dormancy to serve its true potential. Paralleling exactly the formation of the four qabbalistic worlds, the idea generates the vital process of creation is formed and given motivation by its corporeal actuation. Innate scepticism confers a prejudicial lack of understanding in our unthinking. In tandem with humanity's indomitable resistance to all challenges relative to virtual boundaries of perception, we suffer a deficit in discernment. Self-reliant processes that typify our appropriate responses now seconded into oblivion upon the questionable testament of another's misconceptions.

Blithely the opinion of the great and the good is deemed more worthy than our own instinct; here common sense is rejected to vain folly, and often where contrary evidence is available. We lose all. To speak in opposition is futile. Words are much distorted from their original intent; for example: Witch, Aryan, Sacrifice, Awe: all now burdened with uncomfortable connotations. Too difficult to process, they remain unchallenged, consigned to stigma and rebuke. Rarely does usage reflect intent, less still purpose.

Witches and witchcraft reference historical terms for outcasts, of persons determined primarily for their maleficence, but also for their anti-social and amoral ambivalence. Few today adopting that title, would consider them explicit of that ethos. It is with some irony that we may note how the peoples described by the term *'arya,'* [158] which implies their worthiness as: *'real human beings, living in accordance with the rightness of things,'* has regrettably devolved through gross politicking to now suggest the singular and equally prejudicial interpretation as: *a 'member of a Caucasian Gentile race of Nordic type.'* [159]

And, despite the problems inherent with both terms, we live in an era where current affairs and politics has demonised the latter (Aryan) and elevated the former (Witch). Long lost to us are those Elysium fields, belonging to the idyll of a golden age. As the true spirituality of mankind gave way to greed and selfishness, legends have better preserved the devolution of culture in European social history, shaped and influenced by the movement of various peoples who advanced and disseminated, east, west, south and northwards to settle detrimentally amongst people of other nations and religions. As a spiritual precept, the term preserves that ideal: The People—merely, 'real' human beings.

Even fewer are those who continue to keep the 'Word' and live by a code of honour and truth as children of the Grand Matriarch, the Ma and of the All Father. Tribal codes developed the rights of the individual, along with the warrior's credo to defend the 'People.' In all things, they served their community, and set great stock in wisdom and knowledge. Priesthoods, be they male or female, were subject to a Priest King and Queen. They established a service to Supreme Law and the Word, though none were servile to it. Truly, this was a mythological 'Golden Age.' All outsiders, seen as potential enemies, remain so, attaining the status of kinship only through an outward Covenant of bonded allegiance. Oaths were therefore essential in the ordering of society, forming sacred bonds of deed within the living word. It became the duty of everyone to execute justice between all people. Grounded in the duty to others, this is true Sacrifice, reciprocity of Faith where all that is needed, will be given; and where all that is given, is taken in troth.

♦ Devotion

Musing on those all too important acts of dedication, there is a particular comment expressed by Roy Bowers that seeks to question proof of devotion.

> *"Devotion requires proof. Therefore, that proof exists within the disciplines of the Faith. The nature of proof cannot be explained, since force can only be shown by inference and by participation, not by intellectual reasoning."*[160]

The nature of it remains inexplicable, and experience alone quantifies it. Always, however, we ask, is the Mind capable of rationalising devotion, and may not the soul grasp 'devotion' where 'Mind' is taken to mean soul? Looking closely at the word itself, we learn that it derives from the Latin *devoveo*, meaning to vow, or offer; *devotus*, similarly suggests, vowed, promised or dedicated.

On the whole, humankind has a tendency to respond feebly to the various aspects of human love. Whatever we may feel when regarding the entire field of our devotions to others and to the 'other,' most especially towards the divine (in all its forms), remains an intriguing bafflement. When seeking the divine, the soul finds only itself, reflecting the dilemma of true devotion. As for Faith, it is, at that singular moment, both sublimely immanent and uniquely transcendent. This paradox of force and form is the word made flesh. Devotion is reciprocal through Faith. Devotion is to:

"Dedicate by vow, sacrifice oneself in the act of consecrating by a vow, in the process or purpose of advancement of self, or of others, in duty and in love."

If we accept the cyclical forces of creation as an 'assignment to purpose,' where evolutionary advancement is also an act of perpetual consecration: life into death through sacrifice, literally and figuratively, then all 'devotion' is, in the absolute sense, fully 'reciprocal.' This state of reciprocal mentation evokes all the qualitative sensations and feelings experienced through the emotive filters of 'self.' It is unconditional, eternal, instinctual and unequivocal. Bowers' statement is a presage of reciprocity, *for* Faith *is* the proof intrinsic to life. There is no distinction, nor point of departure between them. Such ponderings observe how our impulse to respond is measurable. As a reaction to a given need actuated to satisfy the self, it is not deluded in its driven desire to succeed, nor yet succumbed to vain affectations of contact. It is perhaps possible, that as we acquire a state of heightened awareness during those particular moments of devotion, renewed, restored and re-remembered through assimilation within Herself.

As the inspiring force becomes the bridge, the need for an external force, once acknowledged in a sensory capacity, is therefore negated. There is no distinction or point of departure between them. Such emotive surges are the trappings of a Mystic and ultimately, remains beyond 'desire.' This definition 'fits' the measure of Bowers' statement shared, regarding the nature of proof. We may posit how the infused force acting as that emotive bridge, propels the devotee into a gestural act, demonstrative of the measure of inducement. Where what we feel, or sense, we return as the 'proof' of service. Experience is crucial. Sometimes, this may be a shared experience, but an experience nonetheless. Experience does not in this case equate to time given up to learning the form, but rather, in giving up to the force of it, known for it is unlike anything else:

"since force can only be shown by inference and by participation." [161]

The Crown and the Serpent have long mirrored Truth, revealing why we 'fall' through love, yet are elevated by it within Urania. Pure desire epitomises 'Faith' as distinct from 'a' faith. In the ideal of Her, we are 'proved' in the sublime processing expressed in the devotional 'vow,' the promissory exchange within the act itself. The reciprocity is the experiential 'uplift,' inexplicable, but unmistakable. It cannot be a delusion, as this is a projection of intellect. The Mind senses its own connection to itself and all 'Other.'

*"Therefore that proof exists within the disciplines of **the Faith**."* [162]

Via these tenets and disciplines, we strive to distinguish what is Truth and what is Illusion, and yet the temptation for self-gratification is so very needful; we must forever strive for reliance upon our senses in their apprehension of manifest phenomena and gnosis in order to resist self-deception. Deeper involvement induces greater reciprocity, but only where the action occurs in truth; if false, delusion follows swiftly, inverting the positive force engaged in truth. Seekers naturally require acts of engagement, proofs of which are vital succour for the soul; if voided, the seeker senses all vigour waning from their will.

"A satisfied desire represents nothing but its own death ... In the state of non-desire one asks for nothing; it represents absolute fullness and peace. It is the flow of life with no ego in opposition, it is the flight of the swallow in its perfect immobility, it is the beauty of the dawn which grants silence to the mind, it is the stillness of the waveless sea ... Desire is a centripetal Fire ... it is the illusion of a moment." [163]

We are seduced by the Muse into four stages of love, each in turn entwines the lover into the weft of the beloved, layer by layer, penetrating all levels of body, soul, mind and spirit. Then, finally, beyond even that. These forms are named by the Greeks as *eros, caritas, agapae* and finally to *thanatos*, finding some parallel in the spectrum of love's form: *Eros; Agape; Philia, and Storge*.[164] Eros is ineffable, indefinite and self-sacrificing (Caritas). A bow signifies a sorrowful longing for union. What makes one a constant devotee, as opposed to a blind man—is the whispering of the Muse. Proof of Devotion is the experience of the marriage bed in which Psyche and Eros/Phanes, become enjoined in ecstasy. The *Heiros Gamos* is the Agape Feast (Eros) between Self (Soul-Psyche) and Desire for Love (Phanes). Once tasted, no other food will satisfy that longing: In her own Gospel, Mary reiterates how:

> *"Attachment to matter gives rise to passion against nature. Thus trouble arises in the whole body; this is why I tell you: be in harmony ... if you are out of balance, take inspiration from manifestations of your true nature."*

It is, a 'becoming,' that parallels arcane praxis, witnessed here, in Mary's gospel. She questions how to identify the primal spark, and is told:

> *"There where is the nous, lies the treasure."*

Furthermore, her teacher advises her, that it is not of mind nor soul, but the virtue between and beyond them. That is where the 'divine mind' infuses 'divine soul;' it is their unity we witness as naked truth, and from this knowing, we derive true will. Others may see 'will' in more forceful terms, as a determination to be, to master fate, desire, eros; yet that need is driven by eros and desire, so may not properly represent Truth. Both desire and eros may prove elusive, yet we pursue them still. Plato wisely cautions his students about the inherent deception of desire, but also of the paradox of desire conjoined within Eros; the substance of endurance, forged in the fires of will, fuelled by time—all is in the 'moment,' the ideal, the blood, the purpose, even service to the cause is in 'the moment.' In particular, students of arte may discover how, even within the same Platonic dialogue:

> "We also find a distinction between Aphrodite Urania, and Aphrodite Pandemia, as the desire towards truth and celestial beauty versus material and immediate lust infested desire. Eros does not discriminate, which is partly why Plato called him, amongst many things, a mighty daemon. Desire is by nature similar to quicksilver, it moves in conformity with ambient heat. Eros is present as the desire that leads towards union as much as he is present in the union of Porus (which represents drunkenness) and Penia (which represents poverty of soul). We might operate with a fallen and risen Eros, but the conditions for this is solely of our own making. Eros is more a verb and a motion that sets aflame qualities in those he touches."[165]

Yet if we apply the will to the advancement of 'self,' under 'an assignment to purpose;' then all acts of life become undertaken in perpetual consecration, through creation's own cyclical sacrifice, both literally and figuratively. 'All ritual is (indeed) prayer.' This state of mentation covers all the qualitative sensations and feelings of experiential reciprocity through our own emotive filters. That desire generates this, and of nature induces fulfilment. Who would not pursue Truth upon that divine momentum? Since:

> "It is a discipline that creates from the world an enriched inward vision." [166]

Devotion is therefore both seed and fruit of desire, since we are the instrument of our own becoming. Awareness is the momentary, yet eternal instant of 'conjunctio' within the 'Other.' Each joy fuels the need for the next; without it, we fall into despair or delusion. All exists within the eternal 'now' the ever shifting moment that contains all futures and past within itself. A myriad pathways reside before us in the fulfilment of Destiny. The strands of Wyrd are as open to 'see' as the tarot and runes, and yes, to some extent we can affect causalities through the knowledge gained in those divinations. But they merely shift the means of arriving at our Destiny. We get to play the game of life with the 'hand' we are given, and yes, we can shuffle the cards, but the game was won and lost before we even opened the deck.

Fate presents the hurdles that act as signposts along the road, markers for events, dynamics, mnemonics etc, all melding together with our own deliberations and choices to create an understanding and thus, a realisation of what our destiny is. In that understanding is release. Devotion is the vehicle par excellence for expression of the inexpressible, where our soul's very longing is the yearning for unification; in itself, this recognises the principle of self-actuating 'proof.' Without the 'other,' there is no desire for it. Existence is conversely proof of its expression. Our emotive response to that call is the key to the 'other' that seeks to unlock within. Truth lies in that exquisite moment of acknowledgement. Proof is Truth sacrosanct.

> *"It can and does embrace the totality of human experience from birth to death, then beyond."*[67]

7

The Quick
and
the Dead

♦ Kharon is the Stang

Returning briefly to the stave, we can see how it can be a mnemonic—a very graphic symbol of The Holy Tree (of Life and Death, Knowledge and Wisdom). The Staff or Stang is a fine Craft example sharing a commonality with other things occult, all attesting to the point of sacrifice in deed and principle. Numerous religious analogies and mythological allegories, share these fundamental tenets of willing surrender by the male hero/priest/king upon the 'Tree' of life/death/wisdom and beyond all. Essentially, as the perfumed altar, the Stang is the active point of sacrifice through the iconic embodiment of the Clan's triune deity.

> "[…] staff [nor] 'Stang' as we name it, is not phallic, but has the same position as the tree of life in your system […] it is in fact, the handle of the Broom."[168]

And

> "The mystery you speak of is that of the Broom[...]unlike the principle and mystery of St John though, the principle of fire is removed, and that of air put in its place…I will demonstrate the techniques of the Broom when we

meet.[...]the star of David is of course the basic explanation of the Sword and Broom."[169]

And then, once the 'gate is opened:

"Hermes was not a god that was phallic, but essentially the guide through the Underworld."[170]

Implying considerably more than is immediately obvious, this veiled expression of kundalini and orgone, grafts and of shifting virtue through manipulation upon the following 'Masks'(given by both Roy Bowers and E. J. Jones). As 'close approximations' he names the triune figures of: Saturn, (Old Horn King); Hekate (Wisdom and Virtue) and Hermes (Young Horn King). These collectively form the father, mother, child triad common to many religious beliefs. Other works by the author describe further the pattern and history of these mutable forms.

Notable scholars have opined that both the curling reed clusters and the arched posts may imply the horns of the ram and cow respectively, having associations with particular Middle- Eastern and Mediterranean deities. Linked particularly to the shifting Virtue of divine light in its lunar, solar and celestial forms, they are perceived in the representations of night and day as the polarised forces of life and death. Images survive depicting her adorned face either atop a curved horned pillar or more commonly as the physical embodiment of the tree itself.

We may speak perhaps of dressing the Stang, and of its Rites of Masking These stand beyond the season round, and relate to the celestial arc. Therefore, 'the' Stang is not a personal stang and why a staff, is a horse, but not a pole.

Pondering further upon the marking with ash, upon the forehead, a penitent act for a perceived neglect, we reflect deeply upon 'Memento Mori,' "ashes to ashes, dust to dust." 'Tis the mark of gyfu: the sacrifice of one's self to the four cardinal virtues upheld within the rite of masking. The shift is palpable, the Compass spins as the keys are flung to the rising winds—gyfu: at-one-ment…the tide quickens, suffocating, enthralling us in its waves…within the 'Thing' all are one.

From the hearth, green flames spark from the revived forge of making: the emanation of potential, the vibrant viridium, literally darts pure and straight, into manifestation. The light of the sun is of the soul; the green light is Her, shining as—'World Soul,' transparent but for His actualised force; flecked with golden radiance, the verdant fields ablaze at dawn.

Other glyphs have developed the identity of the 'Tree of Life': primarily, the triangle and the tau cross. Another, yet more significant, is the ankh, referred to as the 'Key of Life.' Treasure plucked from the inspiring culture of the Indus Valley has gifted a beautiful seal portraying, very simply, the motif of a bull deity in front of a horned female deity within a tree whose branches curve sympathetically up and outwards as horns. Cedars and other sacred trees were the oracles of Heaven and Earth; moreover a certain kind of divination known as phyllomancy (favoured by both E.J.J. & R.B.) where the divine breath speaks as the winds rustling through the leaves, imparting its secrets and wisdoms.

Sophia, as the Midnight Sun, longs for unity within the fire of the forge. Her celestial veil, dances freely o'er hill and dale, flashing, spiralling in the mists, boldly crystalline in its glare. Holding within itself the fractal prism, all around plummets into darkness before the Emerald Crown. It beholds the spark within the Lamp. He is Her Dark Light personified; His light shines in extension—lux et tenebris——light in extension—Hail daughter of Nyx, for thy bright gift of flame to our kind. Na'maah to Tubal. Nike to Prometheus, Prometheus to humanity;

When traditional material is transplanted, taking root elsewhere, away from its origins, the people taking up that tradition must adapt their own local folklore in line with it. On alien shores, they must ponder upon other trees to gain their whispering tongue. Then only, are they fit for the cutting of Staves and Stangs, wands and knife shafts.

Context reveals everything it is said, and the primal gods of the archaic world are herein presented, preserving the cosmology of the 'Clan of Tubal Cain' and its eschatology inviting true seekers to walk again in Eden. How we achieve that sublime destiny is a task that focuses upon the Stang as a pivotal key.

There is one Clan Stang only. All poles serve as vehicles of mind and spirit, they have many levels of purpose that includes elements of philosophy. So there is, in addition to that, several totemic stangs and personal stangs all serving in their own way to complete a circuit of virtue alongside a seasonal narrative. As Psyche on her journey to the underworld, you will reach the lifeless river (Akheron) over which Kharon presides.

> *"He peremptorily demands the fare, and when he receives it he transports travellers on his stitched-up craft over to the further shore. (So even among the dead, greed enjoys its life; even that great god Charon, who gathers taxes for Dis (Haides), does not do anything for nothing."*[171]

Tradition of coinage for the Ferryman might explain why two fates are necessary. The first is probably to pay for safe passage across the river; the second is for a swift and prompt return journey. These are matters of concern, for the *mystes* is expected to return to the manifest plane in order to continue their soul's journey. This could, again be reflected in the symbol of the maze, so often associated with initiatory caves, entrances to the subterranean chthonic realms, and graves (often burial mounds).

"In effect then the grave becomes the gateway between the physical earth and the spirit world of the Goddess"—E. J. J.

The Ferryman performs the role of psychopomp for the dead but, more importantly, he completes that cycle as initiator of rebirth into the mysteries and of the delivery and guidance to those who experience *'fanad'* (annihilation of the Self when living). Remembering that this ferry goes both ways, there is another, parallel tradition that places a coin one in the mouth in addition to the coins placed over the eyes. Related to the breath, Ruach, this other, most curious custom may have been Christianised. In addressing specific tenets of the Last Rites whence the Eucharist is given up to the gaping cavern of the mouth, this serves as provision for the perilous journey ahead. Coin is of low denomination, suggesting that the 'profane value' was not intrinsically important to its placement, nor inimical. The use of coinage, or rudimentary metal currency, is apparently as early as the introduction of money. This suggests that, with a view from the mysteries, it may have had more to do with the metallurgical process, alchemy, involved in transformation of ore into metal, symbolising the purification of the soul in preparedness for its journey. The coin then assumes the act and value of the sacrifice of life, of free will etc., of the dying or dead soul, the price paid by the initiate into the Eleusinian mysteries.

In terms of the practice, it seems this occurs in a small percentage of graves within any culture. However, it is a long established and widespread practice, spanning from the 5th Century BC into the medieval period, suggesting that it is, perhaps, a cultic rite observed predominantly by initiates. Entry into the mystery of 'death' (especially during life) originally transpired through the *obal* for Kharon; but this morbid toll signified treasure, and was not necessarily coin, and not always copper. It very much depended upon the wealth of the deceased or the traveller to

Hades' Realm. Gifted to the *'quick and the dead,'* soul pennies all, by eye, hand or tongue. Two pennies to anchor the wandering dead, one for Kharon's boat, and one for the devil himself, as Dragon Lord and Hoarder of all Treasures.

We may attribute many symbolic representations to it, dependent upon individual practise and the attendant, requisite Mythos and Cosmology assigned to that. Of course, this raises the question, should we then retain archaic superstition when we have in all other senses, evolved away from it. Even the sophistication of beautiful classical texts supersede many that are extant or even revived. Our understanding of them during their evolutionary undertaking may, shadow and blight our gnosis, unless we address the issue of superstition for its own sake. We need not retain irrelevant superstitions to avoid the pitfalls of literalism, though we most certainly do need to explore this particular mystery laterally, drawing on the resources of instinct balanced by intuition.

The Mind often fools, where the heart does not; for the throbbing heart knows the way. Gyfu is the treasure one values most. The beast is Mind, swift and sharp, or dull and slow. He carries the unbidden keys of time and place for that voluntary fee. Blind superstition impedes the way even as She calls us beyond it. To consider the 'gift' in terms of coinage is almost a blasphemy. Spirit has no need of coin, and yet coin is given. Spirit shifts for itself, and yet the boatman comes. We must remember always, that the fee is paid if beast be slain or not; the crossing is the challenge to present like the grail knight the right change. If we think in terms of the questions put to the Grail knights, they are invariably exchanged amidst the penetrating silence the presence of Kharon imbues.

Death has no voice, for silent is She ... we may speak not of those things we see not, the matter of life is but death, yet the 'matter' of death is a mystery ...

Even so, when that final shadow falls, and fall it will, what is money but an empty gesture to pay the bearer a promissory note. It is always hoped that archaic forms should develop and evolve; all that is redundant must be shaken free, sloughed off to reveal the fresh, shining layers beneath the cumulative dust of age and neglect. No crossing is possible without Kharon; spectral boatman, he fulfils his own doom, ever the journeyman, ever watchful. His liminal existence is often unmarked these days, where few traditions for the dead endure. Swiftly the boatman calls, and as silently, departs. What use then of the 'spoils of life'? Treasure, nought but an empty gesture to enrich the bearer, a proscribed wealth, a borrowed amount, is loaned for the term of one's life, and no longer. And what is death but a culling of this debt. There are no pockets in a shroud. Principle tenets of the Craft hope that archaic forms should develop and evolve; all that is redundant must be shaken free, sloughed off to reveal the fresh, shining layers beneath the cumulative dust of age and neglect.

Placing pennies on the eyes rather than in the mouth became a Victorian observance, a superstition borne of their macabre fascination for all that lived and walked abroad in death. As death occurred, all time must pause. Clocks stopped by hand, ensured the suspension of normality, severing all links to life. Rationale must likewise be suspended, as superstition abounds where death and the soul part company. Eyes cast an inner and outer mystique as windows into and a mirror away from the body. As portals, the seeing lens must be blinded, lest it cast forth its soul into another, or become trapped in an unveiled mirror by their own reflection. The survival of this organism requires the happy symbiosis of an artful graft. We need not assert the burden of literality where cold empiricism dances on the shadows of instinct, abandoned by intuition. No, we must shift into the wind, and ride with absolute conviction that we know nothing and everything is possible.

Never more is the will the strongest to grasp life, than in the moment of death, and all desire must be thwarted, lest the lamenting soul wander forever, lost in the other. The way of death is the only pathway they must follow, onto the halls of their ancestral making, should they be so prepared. The passage of the soul from the mouth to the eyes, as breath, became sight, when the kiss became fear, generated the catalyst for the transmutation of belief and practise. Should we approach this mystery as one unbound by restrictive Arcanum…perhaps. Our sophistication has possibly rendered all such theorem as outmoded, consigned to quaint histories, offering little today by way of gnosis. More to Muse upon…always

"for she is the ferry, the journey and the destination" [172]

A river is rather like the crossroads in that one faces three choices:

♦ Follow it upstream to the source.

♦ Cross it to the other side, or

♦ Continue along it toward the ocean (into the abyss), conflating meanings of symbolism and traditions somewhat.

By way of connecting the coin in the mouth with the river,

"In Hebrew Kabbalah, this 'river of life' corresponds to the 'channels' of the sephirothic tree, by which the influences of the 'upper world' are transmitted to the 'lower world,' and which are also directly related to the Shekinah." [173]

Of further interest here, is Bowers' reference within the Joe Wilson letters, to the salmon as the sacred fish of Wisdom.[174] The salmon returns upstream to its place of birth only to die in the act of fertilisation. Guenon suggests that to 'cross over' the 'river of death' is to attain Nirvana:

"The state of being that is definitely liberated from death."

160

Another crucial tenet of 'The Cochrane Tradition,' concerns his belief that the soul of a witch, could cross and re-cross this river, as the 'quick' among the dead (that is with conscious awareness). Conversely, that of a 'pagan,' (whom he considered to be non-initiates of the true Mysteries), would remain with the living, as the 'dead' in carnate form (that is), to be asleep, dead to the mystes. He also believed they would thereafter be limited as discarnate beings within the 'Land of the Dead.'

In a letter written to the occultist William Gray, Bowers refers to his firm belief that the soul of a witch returns from across the 'river' to reclaim the 'quick,' moving on to other lives.

"Now around the Castle winds the River or Time. It is this that distinguishes us from the quick (living) and the dead. . . It is also the beginning of power and distinguishing mark between a witch and a pagan, since the witch crosses the River [while] a pagan remains with the quick."[175]

Implying that, in this appended sense, a witch is able to traverse the realms of life, death and beyond quite freely, at will, being the leaper between—essentially *'outside time'*... but the pagan cannot. But why should the soul of a witch be different from any other soul? In a sense, of course it is not, but a key work within the Craft is that which 'trains' the soul to knowingly enter its re- incarnation rather than an unknown rebirth. This unknown state is likened to death, or sleep. So we have to ask: does Valhalla, Paradise or Heaven exist as the eternal resting places for millions of souls? And is there yet another resting place along the spiral path from whence the unknowing soul is reborn time and time again until it becomes spiritually aware of itself along the spiral path to the Godhead for all such seeking souls to find? This is the Mystery Robert Cochrane expressed through the line: *"that desire to survive created the pathway into the Otherworld."* From this, the soul of a witch is able to find their way 'Home' again, responding: *"like to like and blood to blood."* ...as one able to traverse beyond both the corporeal and metaphysical bounds of the *'quick and the dead'* respectively, in life and after death.

Within The Clan of Tubal Cain, the third and most important transformation occurs when we start to follow the path of the shaman-witch whose soul is trained in trance-working. Reaching out across the river and into the Otherworld, that soul defies the laws of the *'quick and the dead.'* It is precisely this same journey the soul must eventually take in death, the only difference being, that each time the shaman-witch returns to this body and this world, his or her soul is the lighter for doing so.

> *"When I am dead, I shall go to another place that myself and my ancestors created. Without their work it would not exist, since in my opinion, for many eons of time the human spirit had no abode, then by desire to survive created the pathway into other worlds. Nothing is got by doing nothing, and whatever we do now creates the world in which we exist tomorrow. The same applies to death; what we have created in thought, we create in that other reality. Desire, as you probably know better than I, was the very first of all created things."*[176]

By being somewhat assertive about our world-view and that of our eventual fate after death, we have the opportunity in this world to help create, then maintain our own little niche in that other reality. Whatever sort of heaven or paradise we want, we can thus generate it, providing of course we both desire and believe in it without reserve.

> *"Conversely, if we believe in nothing, then 'nothing' is what we will get after death. To this end, specific symbols and rituals help to reinforce our beliefs and maintain the continuity of our particular tradition, which will preserve that Otherworld place where our souls take respite while awaiting rebirth. Everything written beyond this point is our way of seeing and doing things. If it helps others to clarify their own ideas of what they want from 'The Faith,' or if they wish to interweave some of this material with their own, let them feel free to do so. It*

worked for Cochrane, it worked for me, and it should work equally well for you." [177]

Likewise, the sickle's upward-pointing blade reminds us of She who will: *"Gather us up home again"*

♦ Death comes as Lover

In the ballad entitled the 'Witch Song' contained in one of Cochrane's letters to the late William Gray, an English ceremonial magician, we find these lines:

"There you and I, my love,
There you and I will lie
When the cross of resurrection is broken
And our time has come to die.
For no more is there weeping,
For no more is there death,
Only the golden sunset,
Only the golden rest"

"... we know that in reality it is a question of the various phases traversed by the being in the course of migration that is truly 'beyond the grave'...To be rigorous, death to the profane world must be seen as nothing more than a preparation for initiation." [178]

Inanna was hung upon an iron hook, generally described as a meat hook. One of the most fascinating funerary practises of the ancient world was Excarnation. Revealing much about belief structures within various cultures, it is easily apparent there is a parallel to be drawn within the descent myth of Inanna. After passing through seven gates her veils fall away to leave her naked in the face of death. Of course, it does not end there; she is taken and hung for three (some texts say several) days on a hook to rot down to her bare bones. She is restored of course, through the waters of life administered by particular spirits at the behest of her aide who remained, watching from the earthly levels. Not to open the way? Perhaps. To 'shake loose the flesh' provides surety for the future. Ashes to ashes, but also flesh unto flesh.

The Moon is Lucifera's domain, watery and marshy, a place where She repairs the flesh for re-use. Maybe that allusion is an illusion, as She is really repairing the soul. With that thought, we should consider the Moon is a gatekeeper, or instead a wayside? Having found them to be un-mitigating and illuminating, any exploration of these concepts intellectually and experientially for many years they have much yet to yield. There is a parallel purpose to this archaic tale, concerning the literal advent of death and our preparation of it but also the mystical and initiatic thresholds, prepared for, endured and won. Similar extant rites and rituals for the application of this concept presents intriguing possibilities. There are, in some traditions, four rivers emerging from the same well-spring in a horizontal plane—at the foot of the tree, maybe? The Styx is one of five. Perhaps Styx is the Lethe. Perhaps the Lethe and Mnemosyne are the same celestial river and the difference is purely illusory. Maybe the outcome, forgetting or remembering, depends solely upon the individual? Indeed, the celestial river is five or one, depending upon the approach of the Mystes; the others are: woe, lament, fire and eventually forgetfulness, on its way to the underworld. Otherwise, like Gilgamesh, they can pay the Boatman and cross all the rivers as one, overcoming the Fate of those who traverse the first five and attain anamnesis. Gilgamesh, after crossing the river, came to accept his Fate. Anamnesis (remembrance of Being) and fanaa (annihilation—a reduction to nothing, while remaining alive) are the dichotomies that challenge us as we 'cross the river' of Death. After all, the primary esoteric role of Kharon, is as psychopompus.

In like manner of Gilgamesh, the Hero's crossing of the river, is undertaken as an initiatory experience.

> "...a matter of the waters that 'flow upward', this being an expression of the return toward the celestial source, represented in this case not exactly by going against the current, but by a reversal of direction of the current itself ... and we see immediately thereby that all this is closely linked to the symbolism of the 'inverted tree'[179]

♦ **Casting the 'Mound and the Skull'**

> "Where nature ultimately fails is that nature is illusion as we see nature, but not as nature really is...all mystical perception is based upon the fact that we go to god, not that god comes to us."

This is a practice where the Skull as blessed vessel, becomes the locus for various ancestral/familiar spirits, having origins within the Craft so beloved of Bowers, hence his adaptation of it into the 'Cochrane Tradition.' With regard to this term, there are certainly elements of ancestry involved within 'Cochrane's 'Tradition,' but there is obviously deeper and wider involvement here. Heritage is sacred landscape. Through mythical and historical origins, connections to and beyond a People are forged—this generates a 'calling Home.' It refers to quite specific methods of 'casting the Compass' relative to the associations given to the Mound and the Skull. That is, re-creating a specific crossroads, a summoning of, by and into that sacred space. 'Tapping the Bone' is more of an oracular practise.

In the *Call of the Horned Piper* by Nigel Jackson, an illustration of a Skull within a Mound, mounted by a Stang. That book he dedicated to Evan John Jones as a gesture of thanks for all the advice on traditional lore shared for its publication. It is also a curious matter that both cave and mound serve as places of 'communion' with the 'otherworldly' Fey and the ancestral dead (also seen as being 'one and the same' in some traditions). This confusion again arises from certain references in supernatural fiction that have not observed the distinction between burial mounds as entrances to the Underworld and Holy Mounds as entrances to an actual or mythically perceived 'homeland,' a place of origin (as described in the book entitled *The 'People of Goda'*). Therefore, the rites attendant upon the use of a skull in both cases would be very different. Between informing and revealing, stands a fine line.

Beings frequenting either or both, will have similar degrees of separation. Termed as the 'quick' and the 'dead; the quick, of course belonging to the Mound or Otherworld; the dead to the Cavern or Underworld. Often they are taken for granted as *one and the same*; but as explained above, they are most certainly not. Traditions may draw their roots from either one, but seldom both. Some other traditions continue to assemble their lore upon error unwitting obfuscation and poor or ambiguous sources. These perpetuate further error and continued ignorance resulting in poor construction of rites and of a Mythos relevant to them. Where we have for example: 'The Mound,' the focus within the Compass will fall upon certain levels, including the Cavern below ground named:

♦ Thuringia for our ancestral homeland,

♦ A hidden but level enclosure, named: Thule, which is the current Hearth connecting us to what lies beneath, and

♦ Above us in the heavens, including the ethereal (liminal, invisible) realms above the Mound, known as Ultima Thule—(The Castle and beyond).

All realms are connected via the Stang, the horse/the Tanist altar and axis mundi, and always part of our Compass wherever we are as actuated by the Virtue of Office, Cup and Stang we bear. As for the skull, it holds the same sacred import as that of Adam's beneath the Mound of Golgotha. Linking the presence of the ancestral line in blood, through spirit, and through bone in filial flesh, through them to the Holy Rood, cognate with the Stang; its sacrificial 'blood acre' is the boundary of the Thing. Our mound is the 'Other' world, the underworld (as cavern) and Hearth, the skull a sign of our ancestors, a particular symbol of our primal ancestor Tubal Cain, and our connection therewith. Casting the mound and skull in all simplicity refers to the Compass, knowledge of its significances, its correspondences, levels, seasonal markers, stellar markers and all 'otherworldly' and ancestral connections. Briefly, if such be unknown to any individual, then that individual does not know how to cast 'Mound and Skull.' This finds extension in the use of skull in other rites beyond the use of it 'in' the mound.

There is another use of the skull in rites 'outside' the 9 knots, and these, of Calling and Cursing, remain the province of the Magister. Because these rites are beyond the remit of the general rites drawn within the Compass, they require the use of another, separate skull. Of course, we must not neglect to note that our Northern ancestors marked *Hallowtide* with the *Alfarblot*. Our lines of ancestry, of otherworld and underworld, all lesson their distinctions in the general Compass, designed, to meld a cohesive dynamic for the waxing and waning cycles of the year. We form the normative Rites of Mound and Skull that concern the Compass proper, designating the virtue apparent of 'quick' and the 'dead;' or we have the Magister's Rites of the 'Skull and of the Mound.' The latter two, are strictly discrete rites passed between one Magister to the next. Both Roy Bowers and Evan John Jones refer to the 'Telling' of the Mound,' which illustrates quite dramatically an understanding of its Mythos in addition to the physical/psychic construction we undertake in the physical—it is the 'Grand Narrative'—the totality of all we do and all that work signifies. It is an outward expression of all we 'know,' and how we may share it with others. This becomes the call to 'being,' upon the Threshing Floor. Cavern as distinct from Cleft, the former being a covered place—Hel, where the dead reside; the latter, a gorge or fissure in a rock face or ground—the opening, literally from which all life is generated anew. And so we have the pale and dark face of *Hela, of Hulda, of Demeter, of Kyble* and of Nerthus. Spring rites universally celebrate the 'openings' that graze the surface of Gaia's form, whence beauteous Persephone in all her forms, *Artemis, Athene, Inanna, Istar, Aphrodite, Blodeuwedd, Spica, Idunna* draw forth life. Karenos, the clefted virtue of life, the Virgin Queen of the Compass.

Roy Bowers was quite partial to cave workings, and this is where we 'see' the Mound, amongst the chthonic underworld course-ways—the subterranean, stygian Apsu, bereft of the viridiant greening of the 'otherworld' of Elphame, of Hillocks embraced by the 'quick.' Contra indeed to the realms of the 'dead, where' 'Underworld' caves and tunnels of Hel (not hell) and Hades (again, not hell) *sheper* the souls of the dead. Elphame is the spirit world that resides alongside humankind, whilst the Underworld realms are 'peopled' by ancestral shades and Chthonic deities who ward them. Herein, sacred Mysteries are worked, sacrosanct in the quietude and chthonic Virtue essential to the Muse therein.

> "*In mysticism that love of truth which we saw as the beginning of all philosophy leaves the merely intellectual sphere, and takes on the assured aspect of a personal passion. Where the philosopher guesses and argues, the mystic lives and looks; and speaks, consequently, the disconcerting language of first-hand experience, not the neat dialectic of the schools. Hence whilst the Absolute of the metaphysicians remains a diagram—impersonal and unattainable—the Absolute of the mystics is lovable, attainable, alive.*" [180]

Appendix I
Definition of Memory
Mim/ir

Memory (n.)[181]

The meanings above infer almost equal state of mind/thought/awareness and the 'faculty of remembering'; though it is important to understand the latter faculty is a more recent expression associated with this root stemming from 'mind' as late the 14c. in English.

Many academic journals now question not simply the etymology of *mimir* but the language protocols and root structures of language from the period of use. They now separate the root of *mimir* with the Indo-European (mer) memory and present a compound word generating quite a different meaning as: mi-mir. Compelled to look deeper into old sources, it is easily discovered how simply 'mi-mir' may be expressed.

mid-13c: recollection (of someone or something); awareness, consciousness, also fame, renown, reputation,

Anglo-French: memorie (Old French) memoire, 11c., mind, memory, remembrance; memorial, record)

Latin: memoria memory, remembrance, faculty of remembering, noun of quality from memor mindful, remembering,

PIE root *(s)mer- to remember—[this one now deemed unreliable and is held in question by current academia]

Sanskrit: smarati remembers,

Avestan: mimara mindful

Greek: merimna care, thought, mermeros causing anxiety, mischievous, baneful;

Serbo-Croatian: mariti to care for

Welsh: marth sadness, anxiety

Old Norse: noun—'Mimir,' the giant who guards the Well of Wisdom;

Old English: gemimor known, murnan mourn, remember sorrowfully;

Dutch: mijmeren "to ponder"). v me (pron.)[182]

Old English: me (dative), *me*, mec (accusative); oblique, from

Proto-Germanic: *meke (accusative), *mes (dative), cognates:

Old Frisian: *mi/mir*, Old Saxon *mi*, Middle Dutch *mi*, Dutch *mij*, Old High German *mih/mir*, German *mich/mir*, Old Norse *mik/mer*, Gothic *mik/mis*; from **PIE root**: *me-, oblique form of the personal pronoun of the first person singular (nominative *eg; see I); cognates: Sanskrit, Avestan *mam*, Greek *eme*, Latin *me*, mihi, Old Irish *me*, Welsh *mi* or *me*, Old Church Slavonic *me*, Hittite *ammuk*.

Erroneous or vulgar use for nominative (such as it is me) attested from c.1500. Dative preserved in obsolete meseems, methinks and expressions such as sing me a song ('dative of interest'". Reflexively, 'myself, for myself, to myself' from late Old English: *mir* (plural *mirs*)

From Middle High German *mir* (me), from Old High German *mir* (me), from Proto-Germanic *miz (me), from Proto-Indo-European *(e)me-, *(e)me-n- ("me"). Cognate with Old English mę ("me").

And from Middle High German *mir* ('we'), compare Yiddish מיר (*mir*). Originated in rapid-speech assimilation of the n of a preceding verb form to the w of wir, e.g. gehen wir /ge:nv:r/ gehem mir /ge:mm:r.

From Proto-Slavic *mirú ("peace; world").

IPA(key): /mî:r/

Noun[edit]

mir m (Cyrillic spelling *mirъ peace, *mirú ("peace; world").

mír m inan (genitive mirú or míra, uncountable) peace (tranquility, quiet, harmony)

mir—world

Already it becomes apparent there is much here beyond the noun associated with a certain Norse giant. The afore mentioned form of mim-ir that asserts the attachment and interpretation of memory to the suffix 'mir' stems only from the 12th century. So, we must be conservative and cautious about the retrospective association granted to the root 'mi-mir' by default as 'memory' simply because of the later noun of the giant who guards that well/body of water. This suggests to an earlier link between the collective waters of 'Urdhr; 'Hvergel-mir' and 'Mi-mir.' a noun sourced from verbs and adjectives that collectively suggest a musical wonder - a paean perhaps? The song is presented as in the *'galdr,'* the mead of poetry as that presence, the indwelling light of inspiration, 'borne' of the inspirited mind? Of the *'self'* particularly, the reference is to the self, the inspired self, the waters of wisdom, font of knowledge, the head, the seat of awareness; the very core of *'mind.'*

Other descriptions lend a deeper layer to this understanding, where the deep, stillness of calm waters induce *'peace,'* a relaxation, a presence of 'mind' in fact. This peaceful body of cooling, calm well/water is in stark contrast to the fiery and tempestuous 'seething' of Hvergelmir. It is then, an inspiring draught, inducing the very 'song of wisdom.' And let us not also fail to remember here [pun intended] that 'Urdhr' means the eternal past, as in contained waters, as in a pool or well, the moment in which all exists, viz, all is remembered anew, anew in each single moment. She surely is thus memory, where 'Mi-mir' is knowledge; together with the third and final 'Well of Wisdom,' (the application of thought and memory combined as) found in the flowing depths of Hvergel-mir, we have the sublime triplicity of 'All Mind.' Both Germanic and Nordic subtleties have been given up to Latinised forms in translation during the medieval flurry of literary activity, especially from within the ecclesiastical sector. These may be better understood as *Hvergel-mir* [source of all life and knowledge]; *Urdhr* [record of all thoughts and thought processing faculties in the act of becoming wise [say logic for example] of humankind since our origin as intuition an on-going and unceasing generation; making *Mi-mir* the body of water that distinctly deals with *"our 'inherited' wisdom"* that is as a people, its own lore and law, its own histories within the greater history of humanity as in *"thou who inspires our inherited wisdom"* from our beautiful 'Masque Prayer. Would not this make Oðin fear this loss of wisdom? ALL THREE are water/mem and therefore carry memory to different degrees.

So the medieval distinction of thought and memory, has lost these subtleties and ignored *Hvergel-mir* totally as the 'Source' of all and of all three wells. Moreover, it is worthy of poetic consideration when we note how the sun, in setting upon the western horizon is reminiscent of the castle of the ancestors, afloat in the western isles. The mythopoeic glimmer of this is mentioned in Roy's poetic ramblings the *fata morgana* [Urdhr!] as that built upon memory within the fading light of the sun; but also, does not also the Pale Leukathea rise in the East as the mirror of that light in Her Beauty. In conclusion then, we have eternal Truth/north/ Hvergelmir/Source; Love/west/Urdhr/intuition' and Beauty/east/Mi- mir/inspiration: the three bodies of water, each of the three fates in fact … of the Pleroma of HER/SHE as 'All Light'/ [spiritual not elemental]. Fire is His, thus the province of the Sun as it fades in the west; and by His Light is She illuminated in the darkness of Her Void as the pale mirror—the Moon.

All forms of wisdom observe some measure of memory, as knowledge is a natural 're-remembrance,' a binding back - to the Source.

It can be no 'other.' It is simply a matter of understanding which 'aspect' or virtue of wisdom is being utilised to each of their finer subtleties at the wells/bodies of water. Wisdom then finds expression within a triplicity emanating as the Source, intuition and inspiration; the latter two being oversimplified in their poor translation as thought and memory. Within our Triplicity of Rites, they each address a unique Virtue whose force becomes invoked at one of three compass points that bears relevance to them.

1. The Rite that acknowledges intuition as the fire in the head, does so through Urdhr, facing West, to the glow of the Setting Sun that carries with it humanity's eternal pining for an awareness of his place in the world and for the love that draws us home again;

2. The Rite that we seek to recall our inherited wisdoms, or inspiration, held as the Muse of Beauty through Mi-mir, is held facing East, through the Rising Moon, the mirror of our ancestral wisdom and finally;

3. When we seek the Source as Void, we focus North towards Hvergel-mir

Appendix II
Houzle

"In the Sangraal rites William Gray unequivocally affirms sacrifice as an integral and esoteric part of any true initiation—that of the self, given to man and god in abject humility. Followed by a 'grail' sacrament, a myth enactment of association to the fisher king, a blood kinship is evoked, forging a sacred and inviolate bond of service. This covenanted rite requires the consumption of bodily fluids as the shared life-force, a pre-requisite for attainment into the 'Mysteries'. But this parallels completely the 'bloedisan', the old English blessing, a consecration with blood offered in sacrifice. Flesh is the body, offered as an agent for the divine, a genesis of a higher undertaking."

"All wise, twisted, crooked horned God. Father over Night and thou who art equal to fate herself. Grow forth as ye hear the summons to arms. Hear the Sacred Bell, and look upon our art. Grief I suffer, pain have I without thee. Superior Lord, therefore be this night together with Thy loved gathering. Bless our lives and the Sacred Bread with love, might and wisdom. May I thrive. Great Mercy. "

This is a rather controversial prayer and has been much contested in the past by those who have encountered it, most especially by Joe Wilson, who had a language expert study the syntax etc., for a scholarly opinion. The results are contradictory and in error; certain words considered fictitious, such as 'houzle' for example, are in fact, proven historical words used by our forebears in the Northern Regions. In our opinion, the prayer is worthy of inclusion and merits deeper inspection.

PRAYER TO WINE AND BREAD (Bowers)

Blessing the Wine.

Madame la Guiden

Thi beth clad et gwynn. Thi art freyed te beth con und kyth. Te brimme te cannes wi boone und lude effend cotydiar. Gyden ic gwynn Thi benison gie to te houzle vin in Thi ferliet Nommo. Mot a' thee. Grammercie.

(Madam the Goddess)

Thou who art clad in white. Thou art asked to come and appear. To fill the horn cup with favour, love abundant everyday. White Queen. Thy blessing give to this sacramental wine in Thy wonderous name. May I thrive. Great Mercy.

Blessing the Bread.

Wisse, crumpling Gott. Da. Fader owre ald Nyzt unt paregall te Fey. Wax forth as Ye year te out horn. Year te Zacring Bell and scry our beste.

Dill a'dry. Dulle a' yave wi' out Thi. Oferlyng Lud. Forthy be this nicht in fere wi Thi leeve menzie. Blist our quicken und der houzle sheeve wi lude, micht und witte. Mote a' thee. Grammercy.

All wise, twisted, crooked horned God. Father over Night and (thou who art) equal to fate Herself. Grow forth as Ye hear the summons to arms. Hear the Sacred Bell, and look upon our art.

Grief I suffer, pain have I without thee.

Superior Lord, therefore be this night together with Thy loved gathering.

Bless our lives and the Sacred Bread with love, might and wisdom.

May I thrive. Great Mercy.

YGGDRASIL

Appendix III
The Law

THE LAW
Do not what you desire—
do what is necessary.
Take all you are given—
give all of yourself.
"What I have - - - I hold!"
When all else is lost, and not until then,
prepare to die with dignity.

Desire is of course about gratification. It is about the sensuous delights of life itself. It is completely subjective. It alludes to illusion.

Necessity is the harsh, biting reality, the unrelenting tide of 'Fate.' This wave of assault forces the hand to act in accord with the will aligned to the external demands of duty, of sacrifice, of non-subjective causes.

Holding all that is given concerns the ability to receive. Giving is easy enough. How many of us can take? In taking, we acknowledge the bond twixt giver and receiver and recognise the value of sharing gifts, though not ones of material worth. They are of great value and must be nurtured in faith, preserved by discretion and hallowed in awe.

Giving of the self in return is the surrender of will, rightly asserted as not being virtue. The will is an impediment to true sight and is given up. Removal of this obstacle is the giving of the 'all'—the self as a blank canvas for the virtue, as yet untapped within, to be stimulated by the teacher without.

This mentor keeps all for himself, that is to say, his gnosis is his own, it is of no use to the next man who cannot walk in his shoes. It is held by him as his guide and key to the next level of his/her own evolution. The mentor instils many things within his student, but never his own argosy. Wryd is an individual tone.

When one lose sight of the truth, loses the way to it or abandons it, then this person is 'lost', literally and figuratively. Without Truth, there is no hope, no understanding and no purpose in this life given to discover the profound secrets of these things.

This brings us to the reason for death. Without purpose, 'The Faith' is dead. Without vigour in life, virtue wanes. So life loses its hold and we slip into stasis, the cold grip of death. It beckons us towards another life, another role through which to fulfil the ideals we lost in this one. And yes, we then choose when and how such a death is acquired. The appointment is arranged by the context and according to the dictates of circumstance. No-one else decides this point in time, but ourselves.

Robin-the-dart

Appendices IV
What's in a name?

Roy Bowers tells Norman Gills his surname (bowers) means '*Crookback*,' hinting at the bow, but a certain Robert 'Crouch' on Kingsley Moor, Staffordshire, built his Church.

This interesting patronymic surname has a number of possible origins, all of Anglo-Saxon pre 8th century derivation. The first of these is topographical from residence in a small cottage, derived from the Olde English pre 7th Century word '*bur*,' meaning a cottage or inner room. Natural and man-made features in the landscape provided easily recognisable distinguishing names in the small communities of the Middle Ages, and consequently gave rise to many surnames.

The addition of '*er*' to topographical terms, particularly in the south of England during the 14th Century, was described as a 'dweller at the bower.' (Recorded in the Doomsday Book of 1086).

Finally the name is also a job descriptive, having variables of (OE) 'Bowyer,' a craftsman and maker of the famous 'Long bow.' One early example was Robert le Bower of Staffordshire in the Hundred Rolls of 1332.

The first recorded spelling of the family name is shown as 'Teodricus Bouer,' during the reign of Henry II, known as 'The Builder of Churches,' 1154-1189. Motto: *ad metum* = to the mark

Surnames sustained variations over time in their spellings.

From Middle English boueer, from Old English bûr, gebûr ('*freeholder of the lowest class, peasant, farmer*')

and

Middle Dutch bouwer ('*farmer, builder, peasant*'); both from Proto-

Germanic *bûraz ('dweller'), from Proto-Indo-European *bôw- ('to dwell'). Cognate with German Bauer (*'peasant, builder'*) Noun: Bowers bow-maker

All very curiously finding their connection to the compound principles of Tubal Cain, city builder, civilizing dynamic and bringer of agriculture. Warrior, priest and leader.

Three Magisters: Meaning of name: It's all in the title

1. Roy: An Old French name of Latin origin, meaning 'the king or royalty, royal.' Roy is from the Celtic, meaning "red-haired", or the French, meaning 'king.' Eloy means 'worthy to be chosen.' Leonard: From the Latin and the Teutonic, meaning 'lion, strong as a lion, a bold, free-man, bold lion.'

2. Evan: A variant of the Hebrew John, meaning 'God is merciful; God is gracious.' Also from the Celtic and Welsh, meaning 'young warrior, young bowman.' John: From the Hebrew, meaning 'God is gracious, merciful, God's gracious gift.' A variant of John, is also from the Italian, meaning 'a clown'. Jones: brythonic/celtic, Yahweh is gracious

3. Terrence: meaning 'from the knolls.' Terrill is derived from the Old German, meaning 'martial, belonging to Thor.' Oates: Flemish, otes, odes, meaning riches (wealth in grain crop—farmer/trader) Westmorland: A name that conjures two possibilities.

1. Until 1974, part of Yorkshire, now part of Cumbria.

2. Also a street in London (now Beaconsfield), not five miles from where Roy Bowers was born and grew up.

Appendix V

Despite the signature (authentic) beneath the typed copy of this beautiful prayer, we may confirm that it was in fact written, by Jane Bowers. The declaration is distinctly feminine, and concerns the modus of the Creatrix. Two lines especially underscore this premise:

1. I am weak as woman knows me.
2. Behold, I am She!

The Ash Tree

I am what ye think me to be
I am what ye consider of thyself.
I am myself and thou as thou art
And will be…time come.
I am Robin, and more of that, with less.
I am that without form
And that without force,
Yet form and force I be.

I am the loved and beloved
I am the lover and his mate
I am the whole and the part.
I am compassion healing pain
I am diamond cutting stone hearts.
I am a mirror without reflection.
I am the well without water,
From which all must drink.
I am words, love and words
Yea! but never speak.

I am pain, grief, sorrow and tears,

The rack, the noose, the stake.

The flayer and the flayed.

The hunter and the hunted

I am the head without a body

I am the body without a head

Yea! All this and still I am whole.

    I am night and sleepless fear

I am fear.

Thou must conquer me to release thy soul.

I am peace, compassion now if ye understand

I am turned about, then turned again

Three times three, times 13 I turn

Then still more, and more

For the hare escape me not.

I am the dead, the living dead, the dead that talk

I am the born, the unborn, the completed cycle.

I am a root, a leaf, a tree

    I grow upon memory of past, present and future.

All things are mould for me.

My top rests in eternity,

I am the breast of infant suckling [Fate?]

My loves kind embrace

Constant, ever demanding

Yet I be fickle withal

For all knows me and have laid upon my breasts

Yet few have had me and they are dead.

Secret I be, secret am, secret for evermore.

Yea, but a plated host marcheth at my skirt

    For I am mighty as the berserkers knew me

My nostrils are full of the scent of blood.

For the dead are heaped to honour my rage.

I am weak as woman knows me.

In that is the fullness of my strength

I am desire,

I am love.

I am the first created the first of all Sin.

Behold I am She!

    (*The Ash Tree*)

The Ean Tree. Written after a meeting in 1953.

I am what ye think me to be
I am what ye consider of thyself.
I am myself, and thou as thou art
And will be... time come.
I am Robin, and more of that with less.
I am that without form
I am that without force
Yet form and force I be
I am the loved and beloved
I am the lover and his mate
I am the whole and the part.
I am compassion healing pain
I am diamond cutting stone hearts.
I am a mirror without reflection.
I am the well without water
From which all must drink.
I am words, love and words
Yea, but never speak.
I am pain, grief, sorrow and tears
The rack.. the noose... the stake.
The flayer and the flayed.
The hunter and the hunted
I am the head without a body
I am the body without a head
Yea All this and still I am whole.
I am night and sleepless fear
I am Fear
Thou must conquer me to release thy soul.
I am peace, compassion now if ye understand
I am turned about, then turned again
Three times, three time Thirteen I turn
Then still more.. and more
For the hare escapes me not.
I am the dead, the living dead, the dead that walk
I am the born, the unborn, the completed cycle.
I am a root, a leaf, a tree
I grow upon memory of past present and future.
All things are mould for me.
My tap rests in eternity.
I am the breast of infant suckling
My loves kind embrace
Constant, ever demanding
Yet I be fickle withal
For all know me and have laid upon my breasts
Yet few have had me, and they are dead.
Secret I be, secret am, secret I am for evermore.
Yea, but a plated host marcheth at my skirts
For I am mighty as the berserkers knew me
My nostrils are full of the scent of blood.

For the dead are heaped to honour my rage.
I am weak as woman knows me.
In that is the fulness of my strength
I am desire
I am love.
I am the first created
The first of all sins.
Behold I am She!

Roy Bowers

184

Glossary of Terms:

An·a·go·ge also an·a·go·gy
A mystical interpretation of a word, passage, or text, especially scriptural exegesis that detects allusions to heaven or the afterlife.

Anagogic
Relating to literature as a total order of words. ie. fourfold model of exegesis (literal, allegorical, tropological, anagogic)

Achamoth
The Lower Sophia and daughter, in Valentinian Gnosticism, of the Upper Sophia (Wisdom).

Anthropos
Androgynous Angel /First Adam, spirit-endowed (created in the Upper Aeons), by the One in its own image. First, Perfect Man, as distinct from beasts/animals/demonic forms.

Ialdabaoth and his Archons then created the Second Adam, also androgynous, and who was soul-endowed (psychic Anthropos). But, in retrieving pneuma back from Adam, the third Adam (hylic Anthropos) was created – flesh endowed; then split from its androgynous state into male and female as Adam and Eve.

Aeons
Series of hypostases that emanate outward from a common 'Source,' as extensions of its being. *The Upper Aeons* are without spacial or temporal measure, they are boundless and eternal. They are silent, invisible and

filled with light. Watery - the pleroma. A veil separates them from: *The Lower Aeons*, that encircle the demiurge, Yaltabaoth, are multiple, and have temporal and spacial measures.

They are visible, mutable and filled with darkness. Fiery – the kenoma.

Androgyne

Possessing both male and female genders and virtues. Each of the seven Archons, being androgynous has a male and female name: (for) Adonaios, his feminine name is Kingship, and (for) Astaphaios, his feminine name is Sophia (Wisdom).

Angels

All angels are hypostasis existing as extensions/reflections of the One/Source within the Upper Aeons.

Apocalypse

c) A 'revealed teaching.'

d) The 'end of time,' the way of Chaos as instructional to Balance and the final resolution of forms.

Apocryphon

A 'hidden teaching'

Archons

Rulers of the Lower Aeons, known as: rulers, governors, gate-keepers, thieves, toll collectors, judges, corpse-eaters. Ruled by Yaltabaoth (created by Sophia). There are twelve Archons and their aeons that form the Lower Aeons: Seven heavenly Archons associated with the Seven planetary 'Heavens,' and Five Archons 'of the sub-lunary realms of the Abyss, each in turn possessing the qualities of earth, water, air and fire intermixed within the ether.

Atman

The higher self. The God Within.

Autogenes

The one who is 'self-begotten' - Christ.

Baptism

One of the five seals: A ritual that may be performed once, thrice of five (or more) times, all of which involve, being covered by water, either by full immersion, or by sprinkling/ pouring onto head, and/or body. Water is the vehicle for spirit/pneuma, and carries the reflection (image and gnosis of) the One, the Divine Source. To be 'covered' by water, one is born anew, filled with the essence, literally of the divine, now awakened to its light and virtue. Hence a new name is given, to represent that 'absorption.'

Call (the call)

To 'name,' to be named, to be summoned by The One, that is, to be sung home upon the name awarded within the Baptismal Rite—this the name the spirits will know us by, and allow us passage through the halls of oblivion and forgetfulness, where time is no more, and eternity lies ahead. It is the ancestral gift, the opposite to spiritual blindness, where ignorance of one's name , binds one to the limitations of the levels/realms known to them, in death, beyond death, and even before death.

Cosmogony

The origin and evolution of the universe as defined by religion, philosophy, mythology and science. These are not always mutually exclusive. Creation myths of the universe.

Cosmology

Historical record of a cultural consensus that considers how the world/

people will end—it concerns the action of fate upon man. This tends towards a religious and mythological perspective; it is an account of the shift toward the final things of eschatology. Man's endeavour to understand his fate and destiny within the greater schema.

Crown

Also a diadem, tiara, coronet Father, Mother and Child each possess a Crown, composed of all beings, from all realms, pneumatic, psychic and hylic. The Crown shines with, and reflects back the stabilising and unifying 'light' created by all names of itself and of their virtue.

Dianoia

Meaning of a work of literature that may be either: the total pattern of its symbols (literal meaning); its correlation with an external body of propositions or facts (descriptive meaning); its theme, or relation as a form of imagery to a potential commentary (formal meaning); its significance as a literary convention or genre (archetypal meaning); or its relation to total literary experience: (anagogic meaning).

Disciples

Followers of a mentor—apprentices or labourers better known as 'apostles.'

Desire

A yearning akin to bitterness, a deep fire that is never sated, the wheel of repetition, a state of stupor, an emotive state of self-indulgence, passion, wrath and anger. Lack of clarity, clear sight.

Eschatology

The study of doctrinal issues that deal with the fate of mankind at the end of time, concepts of the life hereafter, judgment, paradise, Valhalla etc.

Esotericism

In modern times, the meaning of the word metaphysics has become confused by popular significations that are unrelated to metaphysics or ontology per se.

Eucharist

Ritual meal—a remembrance of life acquired through divine sacrifice,—gyfu. Primarily of Bread and Wine, it is another of the Five Seals, a sacramental meal, shared with and as, the presence of the divine. Continues the work of baptism, keeping body and soul in a 'state of readiness.' Salt for Sophia.

Fate

A gnostic premise states that Fate was created by The Archons to 'bind' humanity to the Lower Aeons. (In addition to time, oblivion and forgetfulness, these bonds, restrict elevation, ascent, evolution. They bind, preventing free movement through the gateways of all realms. It is the measure of one's life. If an hallucination is experienced as the patient is falling asleep then it is described as hypnagogic.

Fundamentalism

Those who are concerned with separating their belief from those of others.

Hamingja

One who walks beside the self, as fate/providence—a guardian spirit akin to *flygia,* but in myth, is consigned to the head of a Clan specifically.

Hypnogogic Sleep inducing.

Hypnopompic and hypnogigic states

These dreams involve hallucinations either before (hypnogogic) or after a dream (hypnopompic). These may not just involve hallucinations - the dreamer may hear things, smell things, and even taste things. Such hallucinations usually last for just seconds but may continue for longer.

Kabbalah

A system of Jewish mysticism known as the Kabbalah displays many Neo-Platonic elements, and some have argued that the Kabbalah has an ultimately Greek origin. In the Kabbalah, God creates the universe through ten Sephirot, or vessels. These are, in order: Kether, Crown Khokmah, Wisdom Binah, Understanding Khesed, Mercy Givurah, Strength Tifareth, Beauty Netzakh, Victory Hod, Glory Yesod, Foundation Malkuth, Kingdom. These ten Sephirot are linked by twenty-two paths, corresponding to the letters of the Hebrew alphabet. Many of the similarities are cosmetic: for example, in the Kabbalah there is a strong sense that the emanations are trinary in nature, each pair producing the next in a process of synthesis.

In Greek Neo-Platonism, this is not the case: usually, emanations are linear, each leading to the next. Also, in the Kabbalah, the letters of the Hebrew alphabet are, themselves, regarded as having some divine power. Although there is some evidence for similar attitudes in Greek theurgy, there they are not as developed.

Kairos

In the time of the gods, when fate decrees it is 'moot…beyond our rationale and kenning

Kenoma

The manifest cosmos. The divine within the mundane. The domain of the corporeal 'Sophia,' – Norea.

Logos

From the Greek word *logos* meaning: word, speech, discourse, definition, principle, ratio, or reason. The term is used in philosophy primarily to mean 'reason.'

Monism

Belief in an impersonal oneness.

Monotheism

Single, transcendental unity of One God.

Mysticism

[*mystikos*—secret] those who through arcane methods recognize the truth within all traditions as different paths to the same God.

Metaphor:

A relation between two symbols, which may be simple juxtaposition (literal metaphor), a rhetorical statement of likeness or similarity (descriptive metaphor), an analogy of proportion among four terms (formal metaphor), an identity of an individual with its class (concrete universal or archetypal metaphor), or statement of hypothetical identity (anagogic metaphor).

Mythos

The narrative of a work of literature, considered as the grammar or order of words (literal narrative), plot or 'argument' (descriptive narrative), secondary imitation of action (formal narrative), imitation of generic and recurrent action or ritual (archetypal narrative), or imitation of the total conceivable action of an omnipotent god or human society (anagogic narrative). One of the four archetypal narratives, classified as comic, romantic, tragic, and ironic.

Mystagogue

A person who initiates others into mystical beliefs, an educator or person who has knowledge of the mystic arts

Mys·ta·gogue (n.)

One who prepares candidates for initiation into a mystery cult. One who holds or spreads mystical doctrines.

Metaphysics

(Greek: meta = after/beyond and physics = nature) is a branch of philosophy concerned with the study of 'first principles' and 'being' (ontology). Problems that were not originally considered metaphysical have been added to metaphysics.

Other problems that were considered metaphysical problems for centuries are now typically relegated to their own separate subheadings in philosophy, such as philosophy of religion, philosophy of mind, philosophy of perception, philosophy of language, and philosophy of science. In rare cases subjects of metaphysical research have been found to be entirely physical and natural.

Neo-Platonism

The source of Western theurgy can be found in the philosophy of late Neo-Platonists, especially Iamblichus. In late Neo-Platonism, the universe is regarded as a series of emanations from the Godhead. Matter itself is merely the lowest of these emanations, and therefore not in essence different from the Divine. Although the number and qualities of these emanations differ, most Neo-Platonists insisted that God was both singular and good. Although Neo-Platonists were technically polytheists, they also embraced a form of monism: reality was varied, with varied gods, but they all represented aspects of the one reality.

Nephelae

Nephelim (plural of nephel) means 'rejects' and not giants. nominative female plural= nephelae

Consider too that plurals in Hebrew are designated by 'im' if masculine, and 'ot' if feminine. Think of Seraphim (masculine form yet of, hosted by Sephirot, feminine force). It is time, perhaps to delve into the more likely origin of this enigmatic and evocative term.

Neter / Netrit

Nature/laws, principles of God. Cognate with Yin/Yang.

Occultism.

Esotericism and occultism, in their many forms, are not so much concerned with inquiries into first principles or the nature of being, though they do tend to proceed on the metaphysical assumption that all being is 'One.'

Ontology

'The science of and study of being' What might be called the core metaphysical problems would be the ones which have always been considered metaphysical. (noun) The metaphysical study of the nature of being and existence. Other philosophical traditions have very different conceptions—such as 'what came first, the chicken or the egg?' The Metaphysics was divided into three parts, now regarded as the traditional branches of Western metaphysics, called (1) ontology, (2) theology, and (3) universal science. There were also some smaller, perhaps tangential matters: a philosophical lexicon, an attempt to define philosophy in general, and several extracts from the Physics repeated verbatim.

The science or art of perfecting the work, through devotion. And the practice of ceremonial, rituals, sometimes seen as magical in nature, performed with the intention of invoking the action of God (or other personified supernatural power), especially with the goal of uniting with the divine, or perfecting or improving oneself. The use of magic for religious and/or psychotherapeutic purposes, in order to attain 'salvation' or 'personal evolution,' as defined by P, E. I. Bonewits. This is often referred to as 'High Magic,' which is considered the best use of magic.

Palingenesis

Self-generation, evolving in perpetuity as a single organism.

Thaumaturgy

The use of magic for nonreligious purposes; the art or science of 'wonder working'; using magic to actually change things on the Earth Plane. Sometimes referred to as low magic. The working of miracles or magic feats.

Thau'ma•tur'gic or thau'ma•tur'gi•cal adj.
Part of Speech: (noun) mass (no plural)

Miracle-working, wonder-working, the performance of a miracle, doing magic, legerdemain. However, one would soon notice that methods devised for theurgy can usually be used for thaumateurgy. While many believe that thaumaturgy (Magic performed with the help of beneficent spirits) is distinguished from theurgy, the branch which concerns itself with purely spiritual matters, this is not always the case.

Thaumaturgy deals with producing a desired effect within the material world, but it is not necessarily opposed to or distinct from theurgy in that the material effect produced may simply be a theurgical result caused to emanate downward from the more subtle, spiritual realm into the dense, material sphere. In this way, thaumaturgy may simply be considered as the visual manifestation of theurgy, just as the body is the visual manifestation of the spirit via the mind, as well as its vehicle. If one is intending to imply that the change produced has no higher effect other than a material effect for the purpose of physical gratification, then it would be more accurate to refer to it as low magic, in that it lacks any form of higher meaning or significance beyond self-gain. High magic would then be used to refer to both theurgy and also thaumaturgy, if this is just a material impression or actualization of spiritual forces or potentials.

Theology

Universal science is supposed to be the study of so-called first principles, which underlie all other inquiries; an example of such a principle is the law of non-contradiction: A thing cannot both be and not be at the same time, and in the same respect. A particular apple cannot both exist and not exist at the same time. It can't be all red and all green at the same time. This includes matters like causality, substance, species, and elements. Means the study of God or the gods and questions about the divine and how we come to understand them, rationalise them etc.

Theurgy

Divine—wonder working. Rites and rituals to evoke the presence of the divine as a conjunction of the self within it, in awareness. A method of creating the environment for that purpose.

Pleroma

The abode of the aeons. The plane of eternal ideas. The domain of the celestial Sophia—divine effulgence. Void of all sense of self.

195

Polytheism

Belief in the ineffable God, the ultimate of many attributes, each manifest through a series of hypostases, and in some cases, believed to be anthropomorphic entities, autonomous except unto fate.

Endnote

"If you want to know the truth, no one is going to tell you the truth. *They are only going to tell you their version of it. So, if you want the truth, you have to seek it out for yourself. In fact, that is where the real power lies. In your willingness to look beyond, this story, any story. As long as you can keep searching, you are dangerous to them. That's what they are afraid of.*

It's all about you."

Julian Assange

. . . .

WITHOUT PREJUDICE

PLEASE NOTE, IN COMPILING THE INFORMATIONS CONTAINED IN THIS BOOK TO EXPLAIN A RATIONALE FOR THE OFTEN CONFUSED AND CONFLICTING ACCOUNTS OF THE HISTORY AND LEGACY OF THE ROBERT COCHRANE TRADITION, NONE OF THE NAMES OR EVENTS SHARED HERE BREAK ANY CONFIDENCES OATHS OR INDIVIDUAL RIGHTS AS ALL OF IT IS ALREADY IN THE PUBLIC DOMAIN, ALBEIT IN DIVERSE PLACES. MY OWN POSITION AND KNOWLEDGE OF THESE MATTERS HAS MERELY ENABLED ME TO ORGANISE THEM TO A SENSIBLE ACCOUNT. THIS IS NO LESS THAN THE CHARGE TO WHICH I AM OBLIGED TO SERVE IN DUTY TO THE TRUTH.

FFF

Notes

1   Antoine de Saint-Exupéry

2   Shani Oates 2012 article by: *'Pashupati: A Cainite Trimurti'* Abraxas Journal II

3   Bowers, Letter #I to Bill Gray SCSIII

4   Bowers, Letter #IX to Bill Gray SCSIII

5   Bowers, Letter dated 27th May 1964 - to Bill Gray SCSIII

6   Bowers, 1964 *'The Craft Today.'* Pentagram (2) Nov.

7   Od's men , a phrase that defines them as followers of the wandering spirit of poetic wisdom

8   Bowers, Letter #V to Bill Gray SCSIII

9   Bowers, Letter #4 to Joe Wilson SCSIII

10   *Ibid.*

11   *Ibid.*

12   E. J. Jones 1991 *'Witchcraft a Tradition Renewed'* Ed. Doreen Valiente 1990 Hale page

13   Bowers, Letter #4 to Joe Wilson SCSIII

14   Bowers, 1964 *'The Craft Today.'* Pentagram (2)Nov.

15   Bowers, Letter #VI to Bill Gray. SCSIII

16   Robin-the-dart

17   Henri Frédéric Amiel

18   Bowers, 1964 *'The Craft Today.'* Pentagram (2)Nov. SCSIII

19   Hildegard von Bingen.

20 ' Tawsi Melech'= Peacock Angel/Peacock King. Or, as in 'Melkizedek'/malki tzedek: Priest – King

21   BSotC – Bowers SCSIII

22   Matthew Johnson

23 *Ibid.* An obscure term of uncertain provenance.

24 Rumi

25 Bowers, Letter #V to Bill Gray SCSIII

26 Letter from Roy Bowers to those of his Clan (ii) the document to 'All Members' SCSIII

27 Bowers, Letter #2 to Norman Gills SCSIII

28 Bowers, Page 99 Evan John Jones, (Ed) Doreen Valiente *WaTR*' Hale 1990

29 Bowers, Letter # 4 to Joe Wilson SCSIII

30 *Ibid.*

31 *Ibid.*

32 E.J.J. & C.C. (ed) 1997 *'Sacred Mask, Sacred Dance'* Llwellyen p155

33 *Ibid.* Jones. 1997 p155

34 Bowers, Letter #X to Bill Gray. SCSIII

35 E. J. Jones 1990 *'WaTR'* ED Doreen Valiente Hale p 34

36 Bowers, Letter #2 to Norman Gills SCSIII

37 http://www.etymonline.com

   Cleft:

   1 n. breach, break, chasm, chink, crack, cranny, crevice, fissure, fracture, gap, opening, rent, rift

   2 adj cloven, parted, rent, riven, ruptured, separated, split, sundered, torn

   3 divided by a narrow space

38 *Document: Ritual Observance to Candlemas point 2 (Part of letters to Bill Gray)* SCSIII

39 Jones & Valiente, 1990 pp 185-6

40 Wikipedia

41 The Oxford English Dictionary's first example, dated 1782 that cites a letter from William Cowper: *"We are squeezed to death, between the two* sides of that sort of alternative which is commonly called a cleft stick."

42 Letter #2 to Norman Gills SCSIII

43 Refer to Images & original Drawings section of Star Crossed Serpent III for illustration of the broom and cleft stick.

44 Bowers in *Psychic News* 1963 Pentagram Nov.(Star Crossed Serpent III)

45 Robin-the-dart

46 Bowers, Letter # VII to Bill Gray SCSIII

47 *Ibid.*

48 Bowers, Letter # 5 to Joe Wilson SCSIII

49 'Wyllt' is a Middle Welsh word for somebody suffering from gwyllt, 'divinely inspired lunacy'

50 Bowers, Letter # 5 to Joe Wilson SCSIII

51 Bowers, Letter # VI to Bill Gray SCSIII

52 Alaric Hall Sacred-Texts

53 In a letter dated 9/3/62 to 'Chalky,' Robin Gynt. ('Monmouth Cache') See *'Tubal's Mill'* for an in-depth explanation of this letter and others in the SCSIII collation

54 http://www.gutenberg.org/files/28497/28497-h/28497-h.htm#ch4

55 Oscar Wilde

56 Arthur Conan Doyle

57 Bowers, Letter #1 to Joe Wilson December 1965. SCSIII

58 In Cain: a cultural myth? penned by Robin the Dart. Further explanations into these myths may intrigue the reader.- in TGF – Shani Oates

59 E. J. Jones. 1990 *'WaTR.'* Ed. Doreen Valiente Hale London

60 Völva (Old Norse and Icelandic respectively (the same word, except that the second letter evolved from o to ö); plural *volvur/volur* (O.N.), *völvur/volur* (Icel.), sometimes anglicized *vala*; also *spákona* or *spækon* – wiki

61 See hag and hedge. Meaning 'fruit of the hawthorn bush'. Old English is perhaps short for *hægberie. hag (n.) early 13c., 'ugly old woman,' probably a shortening of Old English hægtesse 'witch, fury' (on assumption that -*tesse* was a suffix),

From Proto-Germanic *hagatusjon-, of unknown origin. Similar shortening produced Dutch heks, German Hexe 'witch' from cognate

Middle Dutch haghetisse, Old High German hagzusa. First element is probably cognate with Old English haga 'enclosure, portion of woodland marked off for cutting' (see hedge).

Old Norse had tunriða and Old High German zunritha, both literally 'hedgerider,' used of witches and ghosts. Second element may be connected with

Norwegian tysja 'fairy; crippled woman,'

Gaulish dusius 'demon,'

Lithuanian dvasia 'spirit,' from

PIE *dhewes- 'to fly about, smoke, be scattered, vanish.'

In the essay, *Women in the Medieval Guilds,'* Saunders lists the following professions women were known to have worked in:

'brewer, laundress, barrel and crate maker, soap boiler, candle maker, book binder, doll painter, butcher, keeper of town keys, tax collector, shepherd, musician, rope maker, banker, money lender, inn keeper, spice seller, pie seller, woad trader, wine merchant, steel merchant, copper importer, currency exchanger, pawn shop owner, lake and river fisherwoman, baker, oil presser, builder, mason, plasterer, cartwright, wood turner, clay and lime worker, glazier, ore miner, silver miner, book illuminator, scribe, teacher, office manager, clerk, court assessor, customs officer, porter, tower guard, prison caretaker, surgeon and midwife.'

62   Etymologyonline.com

Old English **hecg,** originally any fence, living or artificial, from West Germanic *khagja (cf. Middle hedge (n.)Dutch hegge, Dutch heg, Old High German hegga, German Hecke 'hedge'), from PIE *kagh-'to catch, seize; wickerwork, fence' (cf. Latin caulae 'a sheepfold, enclosure,' Gaulish caio 'circumvallation,' Welsh cae 'fence, hedge'). Related to Old English haga 'enclosure, hedge' (see haw). Figurative sense of 'boundary, barrier' is from mid-14c. Prefixed to any word, it 'notes something mean, vile, of the lowest class [Johnson], from contemptuous attributive sense of: 'plying one's trade under a hedge' (hedge-priest, hedge-lawyer, hedge-wench, etc.), a usage attested from 1530s. haw (n.) 'enclosure,' Old English haga 'enclosure, hedge,' from Proto-Germanic *hag- (cf. Old Norse hagi, Old Saxon hago, German Hag 'hedge;' Middle Dutch hage, Dutch haag, as in the city name - The Hague).

63   Shani Oates, 2010 *Tubelos Green Fire'* Mandrake of Oxford

64   *Ibid.*

65   Pers. Corres with E. J. Jones

66   *Ibid.*

67   Ulric Gestumblindi Goding

68   Candlemas Rite Letter addendum to Bill Gray SCSIII

69   Robin-the-dart

70   Bowers # 3 to Joe Wilson SCSIII

71   Bowers, Letter #V to Bill Gray SCSIII

72   Bowers, Letter #II to Bill Gray SCSIII

73   E. J. Jones, 23rd August 1996, pers. corres

74   Bowers, Letter # IX to Bill Gray

75   Bowers, Letter # 2 to Joe Wilson

76   *'A Scottish Dictionary 1700-1860'* C. Innes Scotland in the Middle-Ages p176: The law of Tanistry — a system which depended upon a descent from a common ancestor, but which selected the man come to years fit for war and council, instead of the infant son or grandson of the last chief, to manage the affairs of the tribe, and who was recognised as the successor, under the name of Tanist, even during the life of the chief.

77   (Bowers) E. J. Jones 2002 *'The Robert Cochrane Letters'* (ed) Michael Howard, p.70

78   *Ibid.*

79   Michael Howard, (ed) 2002 *'The Robert Cochrane Letters'* p73

80   E. J. Jones. pers. corr. 1998

81   Ibid.

82   Better understood in folk terms as a centralised group mind/soul – Egeregore

83   Bowers, Letter #4 to Joe Wilson, he describes how in the past a 'maid' was used to scry, whilst in trance, onlookers would gaze upon the reflective silver moon upon her dark cloak, accentuated by the firelight. SCSIII

84   Bowers, Letter #6 to Joe Wilson. SCSIII

85   E. J. Jones 2000 *'The Roebuck in the Thicket'* (ed) Michael Howard Capall Bann p89

86   Bowers, Letter #4 to Joe Wilson. SCSIII

87   E. J. Jones, November 1999, pers. corres.

88   *'Letters to Sir Walter Scott'* by John Macculloch

89   Bowers, Letter #2 to Bill Gray SCSIII

90   *'A Scottish Dictionary 1700-1860'* C. Innes Scotland in the Middle-Ages; TANIST, n. Also -er, †tainist-. Celtic Law: the successor to a Celtic king or chief (of Ireland or Scotland), elected during his predecessor's lifetime from within certain degrees of kinship. See J. Cameron 'Celtic Law' (1937) 179, J. H. Stevenson in Sc. Hist. Review XXV. 1, A. O. Anderson ibid. 382). Hence *tanistic*, of a *tanist*, tanistry, the system of succession through a tanist, the office of tanist, taniststone, a stone on which a tanist was said to have stood to be sworn into his office. Hist.

91   *'A Scottish Dictionary 1700 –1860'* Sc. 1885 Blackwood's Mag. (July) 117: *A more characteristic specimen of a Tanist stone may be seen on* the top of DunAdd, a rocky isolated hill about 200 feet high, in Argyleshire, *not far from Ardrishaig. On a smooth, flat piece of rock which protrudes above the surface there is carved the mark of a right foot covered with* the old cuaran or thick stocking, eleven inches long and four inches and *a half broad*. And also: Sc. 1851 D. Wilson Prehist. Annals. (1863) I. 140: Other monoliths are probably the Tanist Stones, where the new chief or king was elected, and sworn to protect and lead his people.

92   Thor Ewing http://thorewing.net/clans/clanorigins/

93   Bowers, Letter #X to Bill Gray SCSIII

94   Despite reticence on other points, Bowers' Aunt Lucy has been authenticated by Bowers' nephew, even to the extent of her unusual interests. Pers. Corres. with Stuart Inman May 2015

95   Bowers, Letter #X to Bill Gray SCSIII

96   Historical summary of peak period of the Clans: William the Conqueror was fifth generation in line after Rollo as Robert 1st Count of Normandie; [In the female line, Eleanor of Aquitaine was fifth generation in line after Poppa]; Richard the III was fifth generation in line after William the Conqueror; 5 Counts of Anjou/Angevin from William the C. to John Lackland; Plantagenets then founded though John's son Henry III;5

Plantagenet Counts from John 'Lackland' to Henry IV.

97 Thor Ewing http://thorewing.net/clans/clanorigins/

98 E. J. Jones often referred to CTC in descriptive terms as a clan of another form or type of 'Hand.' Pers. Corres.

99 Bowers, Letter # 2 to Joe Wilson. SCSIII

100 Bowers, quoting form an obscure Nursery Rhyme Letter #1 to Joe Wilson *SCSIII* (ed) Mike Howard Capall Bann p17

101 Bowers Letter # IX to Bill Gray SCSIII

102 Bowers Letter #5 to Bill Gray SCSIII

103 E. J. Jones referred to Bowers' wife, the Lady of the Clan, and its Maid, "as the *fifth* of her generation." Pers. Corres. 1998/9

104 Bowers, Letter #X to Bill Gray SCSIII

105 Bowers, Letter #2 to Joe Wilson 12th Night 1966 Cited by Bowers to emphasise the importance and value of chieftains, that is the tradition of worthy allies, though sub-ordinate to himself, are worthy men in charge of their own people, and who may be called upon when needed.

106 *'Letters to Sir Walter Scott'* by John Macculloch

107 Having both Norse and Germanic origins.

108 Norman C Milne, 'Scottish Culture and Traditions' by p16

109 Bowers, 1964. *'The Craft Today'* (by Robert Cochrane) Pentagram (2) Nov.

110 Thor Ewing http://thorewing.net/clans/clanorigins/

111 Thor Ewing http://thorewing.net/clans/clanorigins/

112 *'A Scottish Dictionary 1700 – 1860'* Sc. 1837 W. F. Skene Highlanders (1902) 104: The principle upon which the Tanist succession is founded was recognised as the old law of succession in Scotland as early as the competition between Bruce and Baliol for the crown.

113 www.austlii.edu.au/au/journals/AILR/2001/37.html#Heading3

114 Bowers, Letter # 2 to Joe Wilson SCSIII

115 Etymology. com: Gewisse-From Proto-Germanic *gawissaz (certain). Akin to Old Saxon gewiss, Old Dutch gewisso (Dutch gewis), German gewiss (sure, certain) from which we derive Old English witan (to know) and Old English wîs (wise)

116 '*Anglo Saxon History of the East Midlands*' p21

117 We may ascertain from the etymology of Hwicce that it relates to a container of some kind, it has been described as a hut: "*The Kelts built in stone and wood, the rush huts that were used until the sixteenth century for milking and cheese making were called 'wiccens,' which is a word that derives from the Saxons, and means salt. It may well be that charms were used in the building of these. Against the simple rural craft it must be remembered that another tradition existed, of which very little is recorded.* This is the Key of Kings." Bowers, Letter #X to Bill Gray SCSIII

118 Eilert Ekwall, 1991 '*The Concise Oxford Dictionary of English Place-Names*' Oxford Clarendon Press

119 *Ibid.*

120 '*Anglo Saxon History of the East Midlands*' p108

121 *Ibid.*

122 Bowers. 1965 '*The Faith of the Wise*' (by Robert Cochrane) Pentagram (4) August

123 Acts of Thomas

124 Bowers. 1965 '*Faith of the Wise.*' Pentagram #4 August

125 *Ibid.*

126 Bowers, Letter #I to Norman Gills SCSIII

127 Bowers, 1963 Psychic News. '*Genuine Witchcraft is Defended.*' Nov.

128 Bowers, Letter #I to Joe Wilson, December 1965 SCSIII

129 Bowers, 1963 Psychic News. '*Genuine Witchcraft is Defended.*' Nov

130 http://en.wikipedia.org/wiki/N%C3%AD%C3%B0h%C3%B6ggr

131 Translated by Wesley W. Isenberg '*The Gospel of Philip*' The Nag Hammadi Library (The Gnostic Society Library) http://www.gnosis.org/naghamm/gop.html

132 Translated by James R. Robinson '*Three Steles of Seth*' Nag Hammadi Codex VII,5.

133 Apocryphon of John http://www.gnosticq.com/az.text/glos.af.html

134 Ursula Dronke, 2011 *The Poetic Edda*, Vol. III: Mythological Poems '*The Lay of Grimnir*'

135 Bowers, Letter # VI to Bill Gray

136 Tri-morphic Protennoia sacred-texts

137 Part of the Isabelle Gowrie rhyme, invoking the blessing of a final gathering in Her bright Halls, used for the Houzle.

138 Bowers, Letter #IX to Bill Gray SCSIII

139 Bowers. 1964 *The Craft Today'* Pentagram #2 November 1964

140 *Ibid.*

141 Translated by William C. Robinson Jr, *The Exegesis on the Soul'* The Nag Hammadi Library (The Gnostic Society Library)

142 E. J. Jones, 1990 *Witchcraft a Tradition Renewed.'* Ed. Doreen Valiente Hale pp 63-65 The outermost ring or moat, representing human labour, is formed using salt. Strange though it may seem in an age when people are often encouraged to use less salt in their diet than before, salt equates with life and work. Yet salt is necessary to human life, and its importance sticks in our language: the word 'salary,' from the Latin word for salt is one example. Another is the saying:"He isn't worth his salt," meaning he is worthless and not earning his salary. it has long been associated in magic with the earth, through the 'sweat' endured in the simple toil of existence. Thus, by making the outer circle of salt, we consecrate our efforts to the Divine Creatrix.

143 Ibid. Jones, 1990 page 53 And where we may say that the 'hound turned up his nose at the cake,' then we are saying that the Old Gods refused to grant what was asked of them in ritual. The 'gate' guarded by the hound stands in front of the "Hidden Maze," and here again we meet one of the most basic concepts of this Mystery tradition within the Craft. It concerns itself with creating a home in the Otherworld.For this "Maze" is a hidden path through the Otherworld that leads symbolically to a river and a ferry that crosses it. On the other side the path continues to a rocky mount where we find: *"the Castle that* spins without motion between two worlds."

144 Bowers, Letter #5 to Bill Gray SCSIII

145 Translated by Alexander Bohlig and Frederik Wisse, 'Gospel of the Egyptians' The Nag Hammadi Library (The Gnostic Society Library) http://gnosis.org/naghamm/goseqypt.html

146 Bowers, 1965 *Faith of the Wise'* Pentagram #4 August

147 Bowers, Letter #1 to Bill Gray

148 See the 'Law' by Robin the dart.

149 Bowers, Letter #II to Bill Gray SCSIII

150 Bowers, Letter #IX to Bill Gray

151 Bowers, *On Cords'* Pentagram (3) March 1965

152 Bowers, Letter #X to Bill Gray

153 *Ibid.*

154 E. J. J. 1990 *'WaTR.'* p125

155 E. J. Jones Pers. corres

156 Bowers, Letter #3 to Joe Wilson

157 Bowers, 1965 *'Faith of the Wise'* Pentagram (4) August

158 Etymology.com (in direct reference to the noble Persian race of Iran–ariya – from the sanskrit by the term 'arya')

159 http://www.etymonline.com/index.php?term=Aryan

160 'Faith of the Wise' Pentagram (4) August 1965

161 *Ibid.* Bowers 1965

162 *Ibid.* Bowers 1965

163 Raphael (The Threefold Pathway of Fire)

164 Agápe (ἀγάπη [1]) means love in a 'spiritual' sense. A deeper sense of true unconditional love rather than an attraction suggested by 'eros.' This love is selfless; it gives and expects nothing in return. Described as sacrificial and spiritual love. Agape is used in ancient texts to denote feelings for one's children and the feelings for a spouse, and also a love feast, it expresses the unconditional love of God. Éros (ἔρως [2]) is 'physical' or passionate love, sensual, desirous and longing. Romantic, pure emotion without the balance of logic. Intimate but not necesarily sexual. Deeper than friendship – philia. Plato refined his own definition: Although eros is initially felt for a person, with contemplation it becomes an appreciation of the beauty within that person, or even becomes appreciation of beauty itself. Lovers and philosophers are all inspired to seek truth through themeans of eros. Philia (φιλία [3]) is 'mental' love, the affectionate regard or friendship. in both ancient and modern Greek. It is reciprocal. It is a dispassionate virtuous love, a concept developed by Aristotle. It

COCHRANE'S CLAN: THE DEVIL'S CROWN

includes loyalty to friends, family, and community, and requires virtue, equality and familiarity. In ancient texts, philos denoted a general type of love, used for love between family, between friends, a desire or enjoyment of an activity, as well as between lovers. Storge (στοργή [4]) means 'affection.' It is natural affection, like that felt by parents for offspring. Rarely used in ancient works, and then to describe filial relationships. It can express an acceptance or tolerance of situations, as in 'loving' the tyrant.

165 Nicholaj de Mattos Frisvold

166 *Ibid.*

167 *Ibid.*

168 Bowers, Letter #III to Bill Gray SCSIII

169 Bowers, Letter #3 to Norman Gills SCSIII

170 Bowers, Letter #II to Bill Gray SCSIII

171 Apuleius, C2nd CE *'The Golden Ass'* 6. 18 ff (trans. Walsh)

172 Robin-the-dart

173 Rene Guenon, 2004 *'Symbols of Sacred Science'* Sophia Perennis; 2 edition p331

174 Bowers, Letter #5 to Joe Wilson SCSIII

175 Bowers #13 to Bill Gray SCSIII

176 *Ibid.*

177 E.J.J. *'WaTR.'* page 14

178 E.J.J. *'WaTR.'* page 22

179 Rene Guenon, 2004 *'Symbols of Sacred Science'* Sophia Perennis; 2 Edition

180 *Ibid.*

181 Look up memory at Dictionary.com

182 Look up memory at Dictionary.com

Index

Lightning Source UK Ltd.
Milton Keynes UK
UKOW06n1419130717
305269UK00002B/6/P